HODDER GEOGRA

Series Editor: JEFF BATTERSBY Series Consultant: ROBERT PROSSER

ECONOMIC ACTIVITIES & DEVELOPMENT

Robert Prosser

WEST HATCH HIGH SCHOOL
GEOGRAPHY DEPARTMENT

Hodder & Stoughton

A MEMBER OF THE HODDER HEADLINE GROUP

Orders: please contact Bookpoint Ltd, 39 Milton Park, Abingdon, Oxon OX14 4TD. Telephone: (44) 01235 400414, Fax: (44) 01235 400454. Lines are open from 9.00 – 6.00, Monday to Saturday, with a 24 hour message answering service. Email address: orders@bookpoint.co.uk

British Library Cataloguing in Publication Data
A catalogue record for this title is available from The British Library

ISBN 0 340 70197 8

First published 1998
Impression number   10 9 8 7 6 5 4 3 2 1
Year   2002 2001 2000 1999 1998

Typeset by Wearset, Boldon, Tyne and Wear.
Printed in Hong Kong for Hodder & Stoughton Educational, a division of Hodder Headline Plc, 338 Euston Road, London NW1 3BH by Colorcraft.

CONTENTS

Chapter 1
How industry works   **Pages 1–6**

Chapter 2
Britain's tourism industry   **Pages 7–16**

Chapter 3
Change and response in industries   **Pages 17–27**

Chapter 4
**Specialist products: Examples
from South Africa and Norway**   **Pages 28–34**

Chapter 5
Tourism goes global   **Pages 35–44**

Chapter 6
Development through tourism   **Pages 45–54**

Chapter 7
Industry and the environment   **Pages 55–60**

Glossary

Accessibility – the ease with which a location may be reached from other locations

Advertising – describing goods publicly via television/radio/hoardings to increase sales

Brand image – an item or a product that is defined by the company that produced it

Codes of conduct – rules detailing how one should behave in certain surroundings

Competing – when more than one company has the opportunity to meet the demands for a service or good

Deforestation – the deliberate clearance of forested land by cutting or burning

Demand – occurs when a high-profile product becomes sought after by the general public

Environmental impacts – the likely environmental effects of a development project

Erosion – the removal of weathered material by the action of gravity, water, wind or ice

Economic activity – when all of the businesses and industries of a city are looked at together

Flow chart – a diagram in which a sequence of interlinked topics, events or items is presented to show the development or evolution of some theme, objective or product

Guidelines – regulations set out by way of instruction or warning

Heritage – the preservation and consecration of the landscape, presented and exploited for its tourist potential

Industrial location – a site selected for business because it is ideally suited to the needs of that business

Internal tourism – the travels, overnight stays and activities within our own country

International tourists – the travels, overnight stays and activities of those from other countries within our own country

Labour extensive – industries in which computers and machinery do most of the work

Labour intensive – a work process in which labour costs represent a high proportion of total costs

Litter pollution – trekkers leaving litter along trails

Market – the people who want to buy a particular thing or use an outdoor shopping area *or* a collection of stalls used for selling things outdoors

Market segment – targeted section of a market

Mass production – turning raw materials into finished products in a continuous moving and highly mechanised process, manufacturing large numbers of an identical product for a mass market

Monopoly – when a single producer controls the supply of a practical product to a market

Niche market – targeted section of a market

Primary industry – jobs involving obtaining natural materials, such as farming or mining

Product – an item or items for sale

Product cycle – when an industry survives but relocates, the businesses and people in the declining regions suffer; this pattern is called the product cycle

Profit – the amount of money a business makes from the sale of a specific product on top of what it originally cost to make

Secondary industry – making things, for example, working in a car factory

Subsistence farmers farmers whose produce is consumed mainly by their families, with little or nothing left over to sell

Supply – how businesses react to demand: when a product is sought after, businesses endeavour to ensure that as many units of that product sell as possible

Tertiary industry – service jobs

Total demand – what the overall market wants

Tourism product – a seaside resort is located where there are basic raw materials (beaches, sea, fresh air) to which are combined various facilities and services (accommodation, food and drink, entertainments); this is the tourism product

Transnational company – the name for a company that operates in more than one country

Transport revolution – the shrinking of distances due to new technology making travel cheaper and quicker

Urban regeneration – the replacement of old structures with new ones and the conversion of space buildings from one use to another.

HOW INDUSTRY WORKS

Key Idea

Imagine you are one of the people enjoying themselves on the beach shown in Resource 1.1. You may not know it, but you are part of the world's largest group of industries – travel and tourism. So it makes sense to use travel and tourism as the main 'case study' in this book as you learn how industries work. When all the business and industries of a city or region are looked at together, we call it **economic activity** (see Resource 1.2). You will learn that in some ways, all industries are similar, but in other ways each industry is different.

RESOURCE 1.1
A crowded, sunny beach on the island of Poros, in Greece.

RESOURCE 1.2
The World of Industry.

1. Think about the people having fun in Resource 1.1. Make a list of the jobs their holidays might help to support.

2. Look carefully at Resource 1.2. Name three industries **not** shown.

3. On a large sheet of paper, draw a circle like that of Resource 1.2, and fill it in with types of business and the industries which make up the economic activity of your local area. Compare your completed diagram with that of others in your class.

What makes industry work?

One Sunday in winter, it is gloomy and snowing outside. You are in a warm house, watching TV. Suddenly a picture of a beach flashes on to the screen. Someone in the family says – 'Hey, let's go there for our holiday next summer!' You all think it is a good idea, so you decide to do it. The TV advertisement has created a **demand** for a **product**, in this case, a holiday.

RESOURCE 1.3
Promotion for a resort.

The tourism industry organises the **supply** of holidays and offers them for sale. To persuade you to buy *their* product, companies and holiday destinations **advertise** and **market** their products (Resource 1.3). The beach scene on your TV was probably an expensive 'commercial' paid for by a holiday company like Thomson, or a resort such as Blackpool or Benidorm. They spend so much on advertising because they are **competing** with others to supply your demand. If they do not sell their products, they do not make a **profit**.

So, buying a holiday through the tourist industry is similar to buying a car, choosing a bank to use, buying clothes or food. These industries all have the basic structure shown in Resource 1.4. Through this book you will learn more about the content of each of these boxes.

For some products and services there may be only one supplier and there is no competition. This is called a **monopoly**. For example, if you go on a ski holiday to the Cairngorm Mountains in Scotland, one company owns the chairlifts. They have a monopoly on getting you to the top of the slope (see Resource 1.5).

RESOURCE 1.4
Industry at work.

RESOURCE 1.5
Chairlift at Cairngorm ski resort.

Types of industry

There are many different industries, but they have been grouped into three broad classes: **Primary; Secondary; Tertiary.** All three classes are involved in providing you with your holidays. For example, look carefully at Resource 1.6.

The quarrying of the limestone rock used to make cement for the hotel is a **Primary** industry. Primary industry is the extraction and production of raw materials from natural resources.

RESOURCE 1a
Chairlift Manager.

I think we should keep our monopoly

It would be better with two chairlift companies

RESOURCE 1b
Skier.

4. Why do you think so many companies choose winter, especially in late December and early January, to advertise their summer holiday destinations on TV?

5. For your last holiday:

   a) where did you go?

   b) How did you find out about the place?

   c) Explain why you chose that particular holiday.

6. Name one product or service you need in your everyday life which is supplied by a monopoly. Remember – the company or business which provides it must have no competitors.

7. **See Resource 1a and 1b.** Suggest reasons for the opinions expressed.

   a) From the manager's viewpoint, give the points for and against

   i. a monopoly; and
   ii. two competing companies.

   b) Give similar sets of points for the skier.

RESOURCE 1.6
What industries support your holidays?

The construction industry which builds the hotel, and the companies which make the umbrellas, and chairs are **Secondary** industries. A secondary industry makes things. It manufactures products from raw materials and assembles sets of parts, e.g. assembling a car.

The staff who run the hotel, prepare and serve meals, clean rooms, serve in the bars, shops and hair styling salons, provide the hotel guests with services. This is **Tertiary** industry – the provision of services.

Example – The owner of a vineyard where grapes are grown is in a Primary industry; the person who makes wine from the grapes is in a Secondary industry; the waiter who sells and serves the wine is in a Tertiary industry.

8. Into which of the three classes of industry would you put:

   a) The farmers who grow fruit and vegetables for the hotel?

   b) The taxi drivers who wait outside the hotel each day?

   c) The local people in the hotel lobby who sell baskets and rugs they have made?

9. For the local area in which you live, give one example of each of a Primary, Secondary and Tertiary industry. For each industry you have chosen, name two types of job you would find, e.g. shop assistant; machine operator.

Putting the pieces together

THE EXAMPLE OF THE HOLIDAY INDUSTRY

When you go on holiday you help to support jobs in many different places and in different industries. The chart in Resource 1.7 is called a **flow chart**. It follows one path of choosing and enjoying a holiday. The TV advert triggers the search for information. The commercial has been paid for by the marketing department of a holiday resort or a holiday company such as Thomson or Thomas Cook. Remember too, that someone had to make the commercial, so other industries could be added to the chart.

Next you go to a travel agent with your information and select a holiday. When you have made your booking, you connect with the tour operators. They have assembled all the 'component parts' of our package product. Notice that although we talk of buying a 'product', you are actually buying a whole set of services – flights, rooms, meals and so on.

RESOURCE 1.7
Your holiday – their jobs.

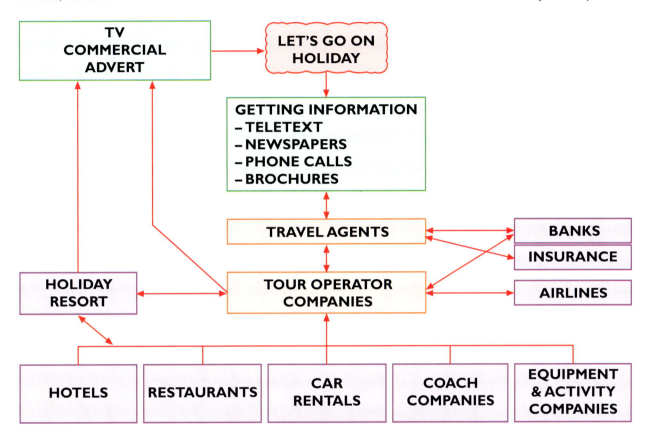

10. Follow the flow chart in Resource 1.7, and for each stage, suggest two types of job which might be supported.

11. Name three other items and boxes which could be added to the chart.

12. The chart is only one way of choosing one type of holiday. Think of a different kind of holiday and draw a flow chart which shows the path followed and those involved. For example, a TV advert is not the only way you might get the 'Let's go' idea, and you may not fly to your destination.

13. a) Draw a flow chart which shows the stages and businesses involved when you buy a new car. Start with the idea – 'Let's buy a new car'.

    b) In what ways is your chart like that of Resource 1.7, and in what ways is it different?

> *Our company was looking for a site in Leominster because there was only one other travel agent in the area. We have to be where lots of people can see us, and just drop in. That's why we are in the town centre. Our customers can come in when they are in town to shop, have their hair done or whatever. We get people not only from the town, but from villages and farms up to ten miles away.*

RESOURCE 1c
Danielle (Manager).

RESOURCE 1d
Andy and Nicola (customers).

> *We chose this travel agent because they have a wide range of brochures, and give you clear information. It is important that the agency is easy to get to. We've come in three times, but because it is in the middle of town, there are bus stops and car parks. Also, we can do the shopping, etc. at the same time. The other travel agent is farther from the car park and the shops we use.*

Where is industry located?

Resource 1.8 shows a Travel Agency in the market town of Leominster, Herefordshire. Two important questions you need to ask about the travel agency are:

RESOURCE 1.8
A Travel Agency in Leominster.

- Where is it?
- Why is it there?

As you find answers to these questions you are studying **industrial location**. It is usually simple to describe where a business or industry is located. So, in the case of the travel agency, you can say that it is located in the centre of town, on the main business street and surrounded by shops. However, it may not be so easy to explain **why** a shop, office, factory, hotel, farm etc. is located where it is. For the travel agency, you can find some answers in interviews with the manager and two customers (see Resources 1.9 and 1.10).

Use the interview with Danielle (Resource 1.9)

14. Why was the company which owns the travel agency interested in locating in Leominster?

15. Give two reasons why the manager thinks the choice of location is a good one.

Use the interview with Andy and Nicola (Resource 1.10).

16. Why is the travel agency they chose easy to get to?

17. Why do they like its location?

18. Accessibility is clearly important to them, but what other factors have influenced their choice?

Use the information in the two interviews:

19. Suggest what effect the opening of Danielle's business might have on the other travel agent in town.

20. Describe and explain the location of Danielle's travel agency.

BRITAIN'S TOURISM INDUSTRY

2

Key Idea

Tourism is a good example of an industry. There are products and services, competition, advertising, marketing and customers. This chapter looks at how the British tourism industry works.

Tourism means business

Each year we take about 100 million trips with a stay of at least one night away from home within the United Kingdom. During these trips we spend over £13 billion. This is the scale of our **internal tourism** – the travels, overnight stays, and activities within our own country.

To these totals we must add **international tourists**. In 1996, 24 million overseas visitors arrived in the United Kingdom. This was a record, and was 14 per cent more than in 1995. They spent over £12 billion, and helped to support many businesses and jobs (Resource 2.1). The visitors come from all over the world, but the largest numbers are from the USA, France and Germany.

These huge figures tell us that tourism is big business. In 1996, one in five of all new jobs were related to tourism. So, in this chapter we shall look at the British tourism industry – what it does, where it is located, who runs it, and how it is organised.

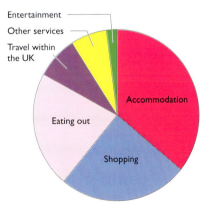

Entertainment
Other services
Travel within the UK
Accommodation
Eating out
Shopping

RESOURCE 2.1
How overseas visitors spend their money.

---

1. For each of the spending 'slices' in the pie chart of Resource 2.1:

   a) Name two types of company or business.

   b) Name two types of job supported by the spending.

'Oh I do like to be beside the seaside'

This is the first line of an old popular song. It sums up how most people have spent their holidays in Britain for more than one hundred years. The traditional British holiday has been to spend one or two weeks at a seaside resort. Even today, about 4 out of 10 of all domestic holidays are based by the sea.

RESOURCE 2.2

Popular Victorian seaside resorts in England and Wales.

By 1900 there were at least 100 resorts scattered along the British coastline. The map (Resource 2.2) shows the best-known seaside holiday resorts in England and Wales. Why has the tourism industry been located in these places? To answer this question, we need to think first of the **demand**. The Victorians believed that sea-bathing and seaside air were good for their health. At first, it was only the rich who could afford to take a seaside holiday. However from the 1850s, more and more people wanted to get away from the crowded, smoky industrial cities. So, demand grew.

A seaside resort is located where there are the basic raw materials of beaches, sea, fresh air and in many cases, attractive scenery. To these it adds various facilities and services such as accommodation, food and drink, entertainments, transport and so on. These attractive resources are put together as the **tourism product** – which we purchase. The resort is like a car factory: it assembles a set of parts to produce a **product**.

Most products bring the supply close to the demand. For example, we go into a local showroom to buy a car which may have been made in Japan. The supply of products is brought close to the demand.

Buying a holiday is quite different. We may use a local travel agent, but have to travel to the resort to 'consume' our 'purchase'. This helps to explain the location of many of the resorts shown on the map (Resource 2.2). They are not too far from the main centres of population such as London, the Midlands, Lancashire, Yorkshire and South Wales. Railways were built from the 1850s. They made it easier to get from the industrial cities to the seaside. The seaside resorts became more **accessible**. Then, the tourism industry began to organise and promote holidays. Follow the arrows through Resource 2.3, and you will see what happened.

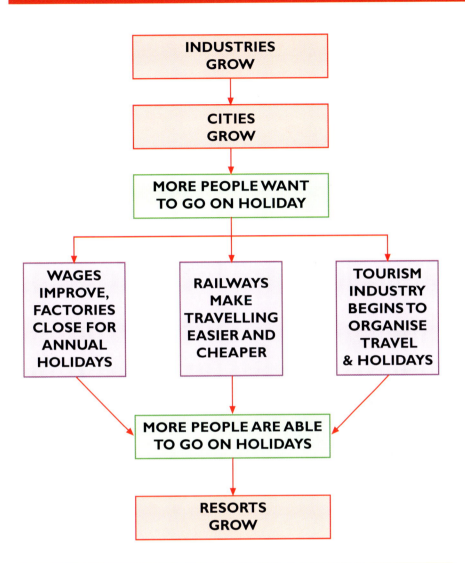

2. Use Resource 2.2 and an atlas.

    a) Name the counties which the following resorts on the map are in:

    i. Blackpool   **iv.** Rhyl
    ii. Brighton   **v.** Scarborough.
    iii. Margate

    b) If you lived in the following cities, which resort on the map would be nearest to you?

    i. Birmingham   **iv.** Leeds
    ii. Bristol   **v.** Manchester.
    iii. Cardiff

3. From Resource 2.3, give three reasons why demand for seaside holidays grew.

The 'bucket-and-spade' resort

Tourism has been called 'industry without chimneys'. So, we can think of a seaside resort as a factory which supplies holidays. A factory is laid out and organised so that it works efficiently. In the same way, a seaside resort is organised so that it supplies holidays efficiently (Resource 2.4). This is how it works:

RESOURCE 2.4
A simple plan of land use in a seaside resort.

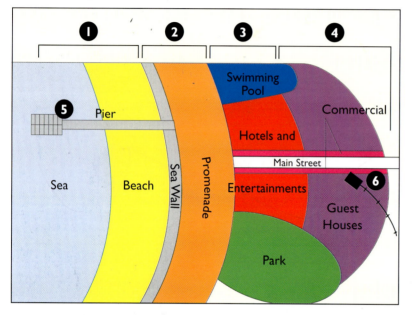

- The main activities of the traditional seaside holiday take place on the beach and at the sea's edge [❶ on map] (Resource 2.5)

- We also like to watch other people, and take relaxing walks. So, most resorts have a promenade with a seawall ❷

- Lining the promenade are the hotels and apartments we stay in, plus the shops, cafés and entertainments we can enjoy ❸

- There are parks, with tennis courts and putting greens, and a swimming pool if the sea is cold

- Farther from the sea is the area of guest houses ❹ which are cheaper than the seafront hotels

- Many resorts have piers ❺ where we can walk out over the sea, and enjoy the entertainments

- Finally, there is a railway station ❻. When these seaside resorts were growing, most people travelled by train, so a rail link was essential

Look at Resource 2.4.

In towns, the value of land is highest at the most attractive locations.

4. In a seaside resort, land is most valuable close to the beach. Why is this?

5. Why are expensive hotels nearer to the sea than cheaper guest houses? (Think of why the hotel owners have to charge high prices, and why people are willing to pay).

6. This traditional land use layout developed before the motor car became popular. Today, most people arrive by car. What problems do you think this brings to these resorts?

The case of Weston-Super-Mare

Weston-Super-Mare lies along the Somerset coast. It is a popular resort especially for people from South Wales and the English Midlands. As the 'Historic events' box tells us, Weston has grown as a typical 'bucket-and-spade' resort over a long period. Today it still attracts about 300 000 holidaymakers each year who stay an average of four nights. In addition, there are at least 3 million day visitors. All these tourists bring in £70 million to the local economy, and support 4000 jobs.

FACT BOX – HISTORIC EVENTS	
1840s	Railway arrives; growth begins
1867	Birnbeck Pier built
1883–86	2½ mile seawall and promenade built
1906	Grand Pier completed
1927	Winter Gardens ballroom finished
1929	Marine Lake sailing basin opens
1937	Open-air swimming pool, the largest in Europe opens (Today it is the Tropicana Pleasure Beach)

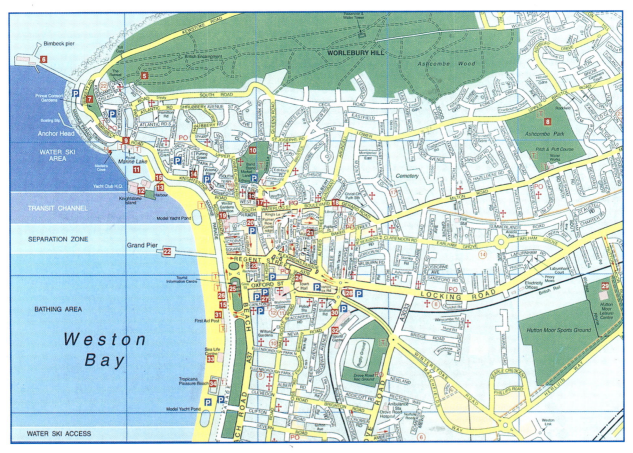

RESOURCE 2.5

Weston-Super-Mare: A seaside resort.

The map of Resource 2.5 shows what the resort offers today. We can still see a number of the traditional features identified in Resource 2.4. There are also a range of more recent additions.

RESOURCE 2.6
On the beach at Weston-Super-Mare.

Use Resource 2.5 and the 'Historic Events' box:

7. Give examples of the elements 1–6 of a traditional resort (Resource 2.4) which can be seen in Weston-Super-Mare.

8. If Weston follows the land use plan of Resource 2.4, along which streets are you likely to find the main hotels and entertainments?

9. Which of the facilities listed as 'Historic Events' are still found today?

10. Make a list of modern facilities which have been added to the resort.

11. Look carefully at the map (Resource 2.5) at what is available for you. Think of the things you would like to do. Write a diary account of a typical day's activities. 'A day on holiday in Weston-Super-Mare'. Remember, things such as cafés are not shown on the map, but you should include them in your account. The weather: the morning is warm and sunny, but clouds and showers develop during the afternoon.

12. From your diary account, make a list of the facilities you have used. Add to each item on your list, at least **one job** created at that facility. Remember that beaches and promenades need cleaning, maintaining, policing etc.

13. Which of the businesses in your diary account are
    i. Secondary
    ii. Tertiary industries (See pp. 3–4 – Chapter 1)?

14. Can you give reasons why unemployment is likely to rise in Weston during the winter months? Which jobs are
    i. most likely
    ii. least likely to be affected? Why?

Holidays by overseas visitors are different

Resource 2.7 is taken from a holiday brochure of a tour company based in California. This tour package is a totally different 'product' from a resort-based holiday. The tourism industry has to organise and assemble a different set of components. Notice how the spending and the jobs are spread around the country.

DAY 1	Fly British Airways from Los Angeles to London, Heathrow
DAYS 2 & 3	Hotel in central London Half-day tour of central London by coach Free time for shopping and sightseeing
DAY 4	Leave by air-conditioned coach for Oxford Afternoon tour of Colleges Hotel in Oxford
DAY 5	Morning tour of Blenheim Palace Hotel in Stratford-upon-Avon, arriving late afternoon
DAY 6	Morning walking tour of Stratford Afternoon, free for shopping and sightseeing Evening: Shakespeare play at the Shakespeare Memorial Theatre Hotel in Stratford
DAY 7	By coach to Lake District National Park Hotel in Keswick, an ancient market town
DAY 8	Whole day tour by coach through the Lake District Lunch in Ambleside Afternoon trip by boat on Lake Windermere Hotel in Keswick
DAY 9	By coach to Edinburgh. Lunch in hotel Afternoon free for shopping and sightseeing Evening – military display in Edinburgh Castle Hotel in central Edinburgh
DAY 10	Morning tour of central Edinburgh Afternoon optional coach tour to the Ochil Hills Return to the hotel for dinner
DAY 11	Whole day coach drive to Cambridge Lunch in York, and afternoon guided walk around the Mediaeval walls Hotel in Cambridge
DAY 12	Morning tour of Cambridge colleges Leave in late afternoon by coach for London Hotel in central London
DAY 13	Day free in London for shopping and sightseeing Hotel in central London
DAY 14	Leave London, Heathrow airport for Los Angeles, by British Airways

RESOURCE 2.7   Itinerary: an exciting tour of historic Britain.

15. Use an atlas and an outline map of Britain.

    a) On your map, mark and name the towns and cities on the tour route.

    b) Draw arrows joining the towns and cities to show the route. Measure the distance between each place, and enter this on your map.

    c) Approximately how far do the tourists travel during their tour? Add this total to your map. Remember, you have measured straight-line distances. Add 25 per cent to your total to account for winding roads etc.

16. What are the two types of business which benefit most from this type of tour?

17. Name three other types of business where jobs are created and where the tourists spend money.

18. Make a list of the ways in which this package tour is better for British industry than the traditional seaside resort holidays.

How is the industry organised?

Some industries are organised into a few huge **multinational companies**. For example, Ford, Nissan and Volkswagen make and sell motor vehicles all over the world. Other industries, such as the pottery and jewellery industries, are made up of thousands of firms. A few may be large, like the Wedgwood pottery company. Many others are local, with only one factory or workshop. For example, Selangor pewter ware is world-famous, but it is made in one factory in Malaysia, employing 250 people. Industries are changing over time. Small shops used to dominate food retailing but today the supermarkets take most of the trade, e.g. Sainsbury, Safeway.

The tourism industry is unusual in that it is a mixture of all sizes of businesses (Resource 2.8). There are a small number of international hotel chains such as Hilton. But in Britain, and in many other countries, most accommodation is provided by small, locally owned businesses. In Weston-Super-Mare, there are several hundred family-run guest houses (Resource 2.9).

RESOURCE 2.8
Transport comes in all sizes.

British Airways
Large international

TRAVEL

National Express
Medium national

Taxi
Small local

Tourism is a very competitive industry, but there are plenty of opportunities for small businesses to get started and to succeed. After all, when we go on holiday, we like to spend money, and we do need somewhere to sleep, eat and drink!

One important feature of the tourism industry is that it creates a large number of jobs. A large hotel may employ several hundred people. A family guest house takes on staff during the busy season (Resource 2.10). The tourism industry is, therefore, **labour intensive**. This contrasts with **labour extensive** industries such as the oil industry. In those industries, machinery and computers do most of the work, and few people are employed to operate them. The motor vehicle industry used to be labour intensive, but production is becoming increasingly automated and fewer people are employed.

RESOURCE 2.9
Resort guest houses.

Mrs Anne Coates (Owner of a seaside guest house) 'We have five guest bedrooms, a dining room next to the kitchen, and a sitting room with a bar. We are open from Easter to the end of October. During the busy season my sister comes and helps with the cooking. A local lady does the cleaning and I have two students during the summer. They wash up, help in the bar, wait on tables and do some of the room changing. During the winter, my husband and I work on decorating and maintenance. It's a hard life, but we do make a reasonable living. We take our own holidays usually in January. We like Tenerife, where there is plenty of sun!'

RESOURCE 2.10
Running a guest house.

19. Many jobs in tourism are part-time, seasonal or low paid, with low skills.

   a) Give reasons why so many of the jobs are like this.

   b) Here are two responses:

   Rory: *Oh, that sort of job is no good to me*

   Megan: *Hey, that would suit me just fine*

   Suggest reasons why Rory and Megan respond in this way.

Does the government help?

The government has set up Tourist Boards in England, Wales, Scotland and Northern Ireland. The English Tourist Board (ETB) has divided the country into ten regions (Resource 2.11). They give advice to businesses, and provide information for tourists, and advertise the 'products'. The list next to the map tells us what the ETB and the regional boards do.

RESOURCE 2.11
English Tourist Board regions and the roles of the ETB.

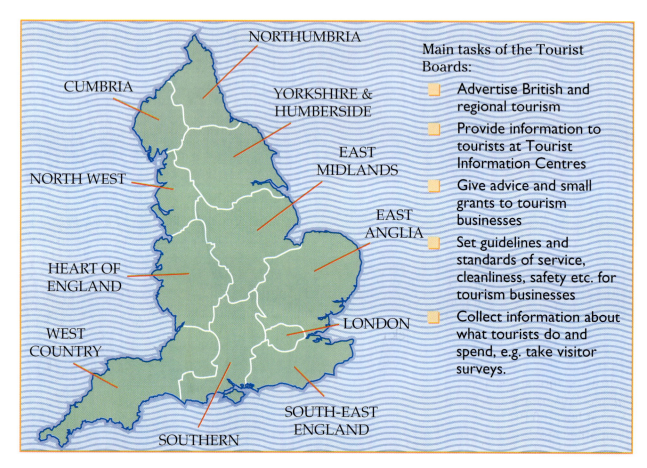

Main tasks of the Tourist Boards:

- Advertise British and regional tourism
- Provide information to tourists at Tourist Information Centres
- Give advice and small grants to tourism businesses
- Set guidelines and standards of service, cleanliness, safety etc. for tourism businesses
- Collect information about what tourists do and spend, e.g. take visitor surveys.

BRITISH TOURIST AUTHORITY
Selling Britain to the World

The BTA works to strengthen the performance of Britain's tourist industry in international markets by encouraging people to visit Britain and encouraging the improvements and provision of tourist amenities and facilities in Britain.

RESOURCE 2.12
A BTA advertisement.

There is a separate organisation which encourages overseas visitors to come to Britain. This is the British Tourist Authority (BTA) which advertises and promotes British tourism in countries all over the world. (Resource 2.12).

20. Mrs Coates' guest house (Resource 2.10) is in Wales. Suggest ways that the Welsh Tourist Board might help her business.

21. Which Tourist Board area do you live in?

22. Name three attractions of your local area which the BTA could use in their advertisement for foreign tourists.

CHANGE AND RESPONSE IN INDUSTRIES

3

Key Idea

All industries change over time. They must respond to changes in demand, resources, technology and government policies. Wherever you live, you are sure to be able to find examples of change in your local area. (Resource 3.1)

RESOURCE 3.1
The former thriving docklands of London are now a thriving commercial centre.

All change

Industries grow, decline and adjust. Just look around Britain. In 1946 there were 200 coal mines in Wales, employing more than 20 000 people. In 1996, only one survived, with 300 jobs. Lancashire was famous for its cotton products, and Yorkshire for its woollen goods. Today, few mills remain. London's enormous Canary Wharf office development is built on disused dock land (Resource 3.2).

Growing industries also change. Fifty years ago, there were at least 30 British companies making cars. Today, cars are still made, but many of the factories and offices are owned by foreign **transnational companies**. So, Ford (USA) owns Jaguar; General Motors (USA) owns Vauxhall; BMW (Germany) owns Rover. Japanese companies have built factories here – Toyota at Swindon; Nissan at Sunderland. Often our government has encouraged the change, to help create or keep jobs. But there are dangers, because decisions made thousands of miles away may affect jobs in your home town (Resource 3.3).

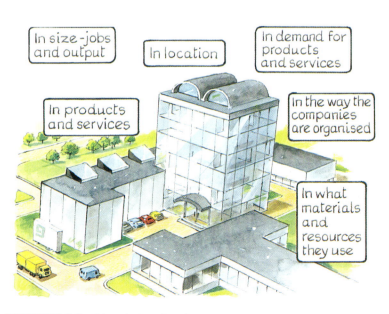

In size-jobs and output

In location

In demand for products and services

In products and services

In the way the companies are organised

In what materials and resources they use

RESOURCE 3.2   How industries change.

50,000 jobs in textiles could go overseas

FIFTY-THOUSAND jobs could be lost in the textile and footwear industry by the end of the decade as manufacturers accelerate the transfer of production to the developing world, union leaders warned yesterday.

New job cuts by leading companies have particularly affected the North-west, the Midlands and Scotland.

British industry pay rates were based on a guaranteed minimum of around £3 an hour. Gross pay of around £4 an hour was achieved with productivity pay. Pay for clothing workers in Morocco — now one of the chief recipients of British orders — was 62p an hour.

THE GUARDIAN, 13-9-96

RESOURCE 3.4b

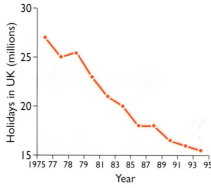

RESOURCE 3.4a
Holidays taken by British population, 1975–95.

	Holidays abroad (million)
1975	5
1977	5
1979	6.5
1981	9
1983	10.5
1985	11
1987	14
1989	15.5
1991	15
1993	16
1995	16.5

RESOURCE 3.3
Job threats by Transnational companies.

One important question we need to answer, as we study an industry is – what is causing demand to change, and how does the industry adjust the supply? In this chapter we shall answer this question by looking at what has happened to the British tourism industry.

Changes in demand

The graph of (Resource 3.4b) shows that the market for holidays within the United Kingdom has declined since 1975. But does this mean that our total demand for holidays has declined? The table in (Resource 3.4a) tells a different story. To follow the story, complete the questions below.

1. Draw a copy of the graph (Resource 3.4b) but make your vertical axis start at 0.

2. Use the figures in the table (Resource 3.4a) to add a line graph for foreign holidays [NOTE: If you have a computer and a graphics package, make a data base from Resource 3.4 and then generate the graphs you need.]

3. Has the overall market (**total demand**) for holidays by people living in the United Kingdom, increased or decreased, and by how much?

4. Calculate the 1975–95 percentage changes in
   i. UK holidays;
   ii. foreign holidays
   (Again, your computer may help you).

5. Write a brief description of the trends shown by your graphs.

Changing our holidays

Because of the ways tourists spend their money (Resource 3.5), jobs are supported in a variety of industries (Resource 3.6). Tourism still helps to support 1.7 million jobs in Britain, but the industry has to change to survive (Resource 3.7). All but the top few of Britain's seaside resorts, such as Blackpool, Brighton and Torquay have lost up to 50 per cent of their trade since 1970.

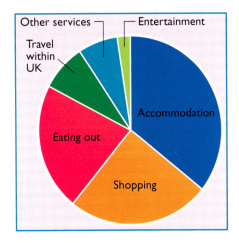

RESOURCE 3.5
How tourists spend their money.

RESOURCE 3.6
Service jobs in tourism, 1995 (% of total).

Hotels, guest houses	20
Restaurants, cafés, etc.	18
Pubs and bars	20
Clubs	8
Sports and leisure facilities, museums, Heritage centres etc.	23
Owners of businesses	11

RESOURCE 3.7
Fewer holidays in Britain.

TOURISM DECLINES AS MORE HOLIDAY ABROAD

Adele Biss, Chairwoman of the English Tourist Board, said yesterday 'Britain's decline as a tourist destination has cost 150 000 jobs. Ten years ago, the British spent as much time on holiday in their own country as they did abroad. Now their increased thirst for foreign holidays has reduced Britain's share. The '70s babies, whose first holidays were on the original package trips to the Costas, are now taking their own children on holiday.

Most of them don't know what a holiday in England is like. We have to tempt them back. Tourism is still Britain's second largest industry. But, while spending on tourism trebled from £9 billion in 1983, to £27 billion in 1993, we now spend 55 per cent of this abroad.

Pam Weaver, manager of the Tourist Information Centre in Penzance, Cornwall, added: 'The jumbo jet has killed the old-style mass tourism. What we have to do is move up-market.

There's too much accommodation in our seaside resorts – but it's the wrong sort. This is supposed to be the busiest six weeks of the year, but it's been very slow. The bucket-and-spade brigade have gone abroad. It's rare to find people stopping for a whole week'.

(SOURCE: THE GUARDIAN, 28 July 1994)

7. Look at Resource 3.5. What proportion of the total cost of a holiday is spent on each category?

8. For each of the spending categories, suggest three types of job which might be supported.

9. a) Use the table (Resource 3.6) to draw a pie chart.

   b) Describe briefly what your pie chart and the figures show.

10. Name two types of business connected with tourism which are **not** mentioned in the table.

11. Think about the area in which you live.

   a) Name one business in each of the categories in the table (Resource 3.6).

   b) Are they small (less than 10 jobs), medium (10–50 jobs) or large (more than 50 jobs) businesses?

12. Read carefully what Adele Biss and Pam Weaver have to say (Resource 3.7).

   a) What changes do they describe?

   b) What has caused these changes?

   c) What suggestions are made to solve the problems?

RESOURCE 3.8
Summer sun holidays to Europe, 1996.

	% of British tourists
Spain	52
Greece	19
Turkey	12
Cyprus	5
Portugal	5
Other	7

Changing demand – changing products

In order to survive, any business or industry must respond to changing demands. For example:

- reduce the price of an existing product;
- update an existing product;
- introduce a new product;
- try to sell to a different market.

Beach holidays are a good example. Total demand has grown, but for different products. The industry has supplied these new products: package holidays in different destinations, which offer guaranteed sun as well as sand and sea. This is a form of **mass production**, which keeps costs down. The result is that in Britain at least 10 million package holidays are sold each year. The majority are to Mediterranean beach destinations (Resource 3.8).

A second major change is that we are choosing a wider range of holiday products. More of us camp, climb, visit rainforests, temples and foreign theme parks (Resource 3.9a and b). More of us are taking second holidays (Resource 3.10).

RESOURCE 3.9a
Long haul holidays from Britain in 1996.

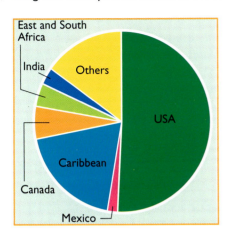

RESOURCE 3.9b
More people go ocean cruising.

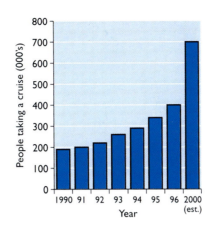

RESOURCE 3.10
500 000 seek Christmas sun.

Top Christmas destinations, 1995
1. Tenerife
2. Costa del Sol
3. Florida
4. Costa Blanca
5. Lanzarote
6. Gran Canaria
7. Majorca
8. Italy
9. France
10. Cyprus

13. From the table in Resource 3.8, draw a pie chart to show the European summer sun destinations for British tourists.

14. From the pie chart of Resource 3.9a, what are the percentages of British long haul tourists who go to each destination? (Remember, 3.6° on your pie chart = 1 per cent. So, 90° = 25 per cent.) Set out your answers in rank order with the most popular destination as number 1.

15. From the bar graphs of Resource 3.9.

    a) How many people took cruises in
    i. 1980   ii. 1993   iii. 1996;

    b) What were the percentage increases between
    i. 1990 and 1993   ii. 1993 and 1996?

    c) Can you suggest any reasons why cruising is becoming so popular?

16. On an outline map of the world,

    a) Name the destinations given in Resource 3.10

    b) Draw a line from Britain to each destination, and give the straight-line distance to that destination. (Use an atlas to help you).

    c) If the average flying speed of an aircraft is 700 km per hour how long will it take to fly to each of the destinations? Label your lines with the distances.

Fortunes rise and fall

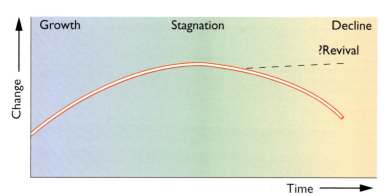

RESOURCE 3.11
The product cycle.

RESOURCE 3.12a
The sun goes down on the 'fly-and-flop' holiday.

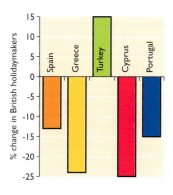

British tourists are turning their backs on the beaches, particularly among Mediterranean resorts. In 1996, 1 million fewer 'fly-and-flop' European beach holidays were sold than in 1995. But long haul holidays beyond Europe grew by 25 per cent.
THE INDEPENDENT,
5 November 1996

Many industries and industrial regions go through a period of growth, followed by decline and a struggle to survive. This can happen for several reasons:

- The materials may run out, as in an iron ore mine or an oilfield. For example, North Sea oilfields may be used up within 30 years;

- Another product may take over. For example, where oil and gas have replaced coal for generating electricity. This has been a major cause of the decline in the British coal industry;

- Factories in another country may make the products more cheaply. This happened to the British textile industry, when Asian countries developed their own textile mills.

So, an industry may survive, but becomes located in different places and with new products. It is then the businesses and people in the declining regions who suffer. This pattern of change has been called the **product cycle** (Resource 3.11). We can fit the story of British seaside resorts to this Product Cycle graph. Until the 1950s they were on the growth curve. Then they stagnated, and from the 1970s the **demand** for their **product** has declined.

Good news and bad news

Tourism is a 'fashion' industry, just like the clothing or car industries. We choose by style, fashion, price, and are always looking for something new and different. There are expensive advertising and marketing campaigns to persuade us to buy the product.

When we change our car, it might be good news for VW but bad news for Ford. When we choose Nikes instead of Reeboks, we may affect someone's job in Malaysia or Indonesia, where the products are made. When we change our choice of holiday, it is good news for some destinations, and bad news for others. The choices of British holidaymakers in 1996 is a good example (Resource 3.12)

% change in British holidaymakers	
USA	+26
Mexico	+236
Caribbean	+20
Canada	+14
East and South Africa	−12
India	+12

RESOURCE 3.12b
1995–1996 changes.

RESOURCE 3.12c
1995–1996 changes.

17. From Resource 3.12

 a) What are the percentage changes for each of the European destinations given in the bar graphs?

 b) Use the figures in the table to draw a bar graph of changes in long haul destinations. (Think carefully about how you can show the huge change for Mexico).

18. Describe briefly what the graphs and figures tell you. Remember, at least one in every two holidays we take in Europe is still to Spain. In contrast only 2 per cent of our long haul holidays are to Mexico.

RESOURCE 3.13
The Big Questions.

British resorts fight back

Businesses, regions and industries can fight back. The people leading the fight in British seaside resorts are Town Councils, tourism officials and owners of businesses. Their aim is to supply a holiday product which is:

- ☐ **attractive**
- ☐ **competitive**
- ☐ **profitable**

Resource 3.13 follows them as they search for a new future.

In the language of marketing, each resort is developing a **brand image** and targeting a **market segment**. The government runs campaigns to help resorts to change their images and products. For instance, in 1991, the 'Turning the Tide' campaign was launched. Resorts could put forward improvement schemes and bid for money to help carry them out (Resource 3.14)

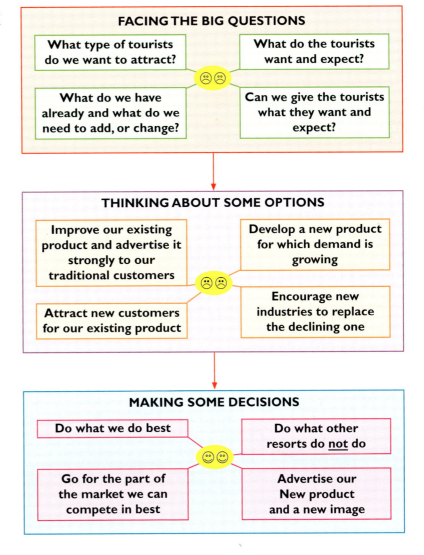

FACING THE BIG QUESTIONS

What type of tourists do we want to attract?

What do the tourists want and expect?

What do we have already and what do we need to add, or change?

Can we give the tourists what they want and expect?

THINKING ABOUT SOME OPTIONS

Improve our existing product and advertise it strongly to our traditional customers

Develop a new product for which demand is growing

Attract new customers for our existing product

Encourage new industries to replace the declining one

MAKING SOME DECISIONS

Do what we do best

Do what other resorts do **not** do

Go for the part of the market we can compete in best

Advertise our New product and a new image

Turning the tide in England's seaside

The tourist boards are giving considerable time and resources to encouraging the regeneration of seaside resorts. ETB's Seaside Resorts Marketing Campaign spearheads this process, but there are currently seven Local Area Initiatives in progress at Hemsby, Weston-Super-Mare, Brighton, Weymouth, Eastbourne and on the Lincolnshire and Lancashire coasts.

For 1993, 41 resorts will be taking part in the marketing campaign. The budget for the coming year is £1 million. The campaign is jointly funded by the English Tourist Board, resort authorities, regional tourist boards and domestic holiday operators.

Here are some examples:

Eastbourne – Surveys found that people thought of Eastbourne as a place for 'Grans and Grandads'. So, a marketing campaign was aimed at attracting younger visitors. This included language schools, where European students learn English.

Brighton – The main aim has been to move 'up-market'. There is a new marina for the boats of wealthy people, and conference facilities have been added.

Great Yarmouth – The traditional market has been industrial workers from the cities of eastern and southern England.

RESOURCE 3.14
Turning the Tide campaign literature.

The resort has decided to keep its image as the place for good-value, family fun holidays. The town has added a very popular indoor leisure complex, and has increased the self-catering accommodation and caravan parks.

Blackpool – Even Britain's largest resort is forced to improve its product. It has recently spent £15 million on its famous tower. There are new conference facilities and expensive 'white-knuckle' rides at the huge Pleasure Beach.

19. Choose *either* a car manufacturer, e.g. Jaguar, *or* a leisure clothing company, e.g. Reebok. From Resource 3.13,

a) Select one of the 'Big Questions'. Re-write it, in the words a manager in your chosen company would use.

b) For each of the 'Options', suggest an example for your company.

c) Choose one new product for your company, e.g. small sports car; new running shoe. Use the 'Decisions' to explain how you hope the new product will be attractive, competitive and profitable.

20. Which of the 'options' in Resource 3.13, have the resorts in the examples above chosen?

Indoor alternatives

One of the big problems faced by all British seaside resorts is that they cannot guarantee warm, sunny weather. For many, the answer has been to build indoor leisure complexes. But just think – if your 'fun' is indoors, do you need to be at the seaside at all? The three Center Parcs villages at Elvedon Forest (Suffolk), Longleat Forest (Wiltshire) and Sherwood Forest (Nottinghamshire) are all based at accessible, inland locations and offer a large variety of indoor activities. They are a fresh alternative to traditional outdoor resort options. They compete not only with second holidays and shorter weekend breaks, but also with traditional British resorts, France and the Spanish costas.

CENTER PARCS: A FRESH APPROACH TO THE HOLIDAY RESORT

Key features of the concept

- A self-contained custom-built holiday village: an integrated holiday enclave

- High quality woodland settings and facilities for family holidays

- Accommodation in self-catering bungalows spread in a woodland setting

- A wide range of outdoor and indoor facilities to make enjoyment independent of the weather. The centre-piece is the glass dome sheltering an elaborate leisure pool complex, with temperature a constant 84°F.

- All-year availability

- Cars are excluded; bikes and walking are encouraged

- Inland locations, bringing the supply nearer to the demand

RESOURCE 3.15
The fun of a holiday camp in a huge glass bubble.

21. Are resort developments such as Center Parcs 'good news' or 'bad news' for British seaside resorts? Give reasons for your answer.

22. How do the Center Parcs developments help to revive the British tourism industry?

Tourism comes to town!

Wherever you live there are tourists, businesses based on tourism, and jobs in tourism. Historic towns such as Stratford-upon-Avon, York and Edinburgh, market their heritage as a tourism product (Resource 3.16). Cities whose traditional manufacturing industries are declining, see that leisure and tourism is a growth industry. So, they use it to revive the economy and to improve the environment. This is called urban regeneration. Birmingham is a good example (Resource 3.17).

The attraction –	William Shakespeare was born here. The house in which he was born, and the Shakespeare theatres are the most popular attractions
The town –	A beautiful historical town along the R. Avon
The people –	23 000 people live in the town, and over 100 000 in the surrounding district
The tourists –	2.5 million visitors a year, from all over the world
The benefits –	Tourists spend over £55 million, and help support 8000 jobs (25% of the local total)
The impacts –	At times, the town is too popular. The streets become overcrowded with people, cars and coaches

If this continues:

• visitors are less satisfied
• local people get annoyed
• the environment suffers

The response –	'A few years ago, everyone knew that our success was becoming a problem. So in 1992 we set up the Visitor Management Action Programme. As a list of sponsors shows, this brings together a wide range of groups. We have these aims: to conserve the local environment; to make both local people and tourists happy; to encourage a profitable tourist industry. It's not easy. More tourists mean more spending and more jobs. But more tourists mean more crowding and more complaints' [A local tourism officer]

RESOURCE 3.16
Tourism in an historic town: Stratford-upon-Avon.

23. Give two reasons why the growth of tourism in a historic town might not be popular with all the local people?

Problems	Needs
• Between 1970 and 1985, the city lost over one-half of its manufacturing jobs	• New jobs in industries where demand is growing
• Buildings and streets around the city centre were old and out-of date	• New developments to improve the environment for Birmingham people and to attract visitors

RESOURCE 3.17a
Reviving Central Birmingham.

The ICC complex extends the Central Business District

Pedestrian corridor linking the ICC to main shops

N

Central Business District

Shopping area

New Street Rail Station

Broad Street

Redevelopment Area

Inner Ring Road

RESOURCE 3.17b
Birmingham: The ICC and the City Centre.

THE ANSWER

- Create a Redevelopment Area, where a whole new environment can be built

- Link this new environment to the existing CBD

- Develop a set of high quality buildings and spaces for a variety of uses, e.g.:

ICC – 10 conference halls and the best symphony concert hall in Britain. Opened in 1991; used by over 500 000 people a year; 50 per cent of them visitors to Birmingham

NIA – Over 600 000 customers a year; 60 per cent of them visitors. It is the venue for the TV series 'Gladiators' and the 1998 Eurovision Song Contest.

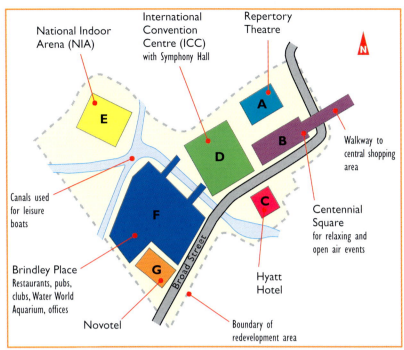

RESOURCE 3.17c

Central Birmingham: The International Convention Centre and other redevelopment projects.

24. Why did the city decide to build the ICC and the other developments?

25. What jobs do the developments create? From the plan of Resource 3.17c. Make a table including all the elements shown, using the following columns. (The first entry is completed for you)

Facility	Examples of activities	Examples of jobs supported
Repertory Theatre	Plays, musicals	Administrators: maintenance staff; actors and musicians; bar and restaurant staff; door and ticket staff

26. Birmingham already has the National Exhibition Centre (NEC). This is near the airport and motorways on the edge of the city. Some people wanted the ICC and NIA to be built near the NEC. What would be the advantages and disadvantages of that location? (Think of traffic and accessibility; tourists and the people of Birmingham; effects on the environment; jobs, transport and commuting).

4

SPECIALIST PRODUCTS: EXAMPLES FROM SOUTH AFRICA AND NORWAY

Key Idea

Most products on the market are produced in huge quantities and supply the general population. But there are also products that are produced in smaller quantities and supply the specialist market. This is the difference between Marks and Spencers and Gucci, between Volkswagen and Lotus. The different types of production are called mass production and specialist production. In tourism, companies like Thomson and resorts like Benidorm supply mass products. Whereas PGL adventure holidays for children and alpine resorts are specialist producers.

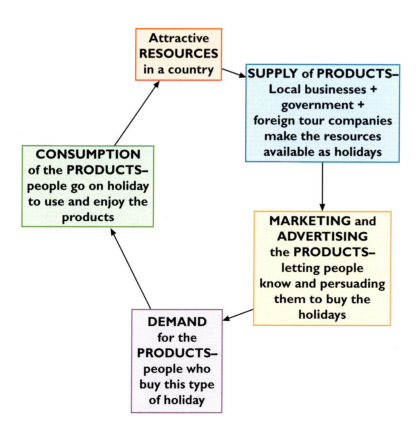

Attractive **RESOURCES** in a country

SUPPLY of PRODUCTS– Local businesses + government + foreign tour companies make the resources available as holidays

CONSUMPTION of the PRODUCTS– people go on holiday to use and enjoy the products

MARKETING and ADVERTISING the PRODUCTS– letting people know and persuading them to buy the holidays

DEMAND for the PRODUCTS– people who buy this type of holiday

Two specialist products

South Africa and Norway have developed well-known specialist holiday products. As you study them, remember these questions:

- What resources are used to attract tourists?

- How are the holidays organised and what do the tourists do?

- In what ways is specialist tourism different from mass tourism?

RESOURCE 4.1
The tourism business.

Safari tourism in South Africa

Tourism is growing rapidly in South Africa (Resource 4.2). Two-thirds of the visitors are on holiday. The main reason they come is to 'go on safari' especially tourists from Europe and North America. A safari means taking trips to see wild animals and birds in their natural environments (Resource 4.3).

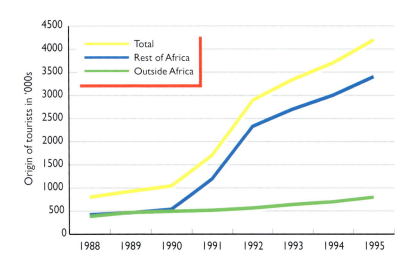

RESOURCE 4.2
The growth of South African Tourism.

RESOURCE 4.3
Out in the wild, tourists in a four wheel drive looking at animals.

ORGANISING THE SAFARI

Like several other African countries, South Africa realises that the wildlife and beautiful scenery are valuable resources. As a result, the government has taken steps to protect them (Resource 4.4). An official explains (right):

We have created 17 National Parks and many more Game Reserves. In these areas the animals and environment are protected so that tourists can enjoy them. We have had to do this because our population is growing and people are demanding more land. This threatens the open spaces that the animals and birds need. There are also a number of wildlife reserves run by private businesses. About 2 million tourists visit the parks and reserves each year. However, they are usually in small groups and are spread out over large areas.

1. From Resource 4.2, construct a table with three columns and two rows, to show the numbers arriving from
   i. the rest of Africa
   ii. outside Africa
   iii. the total numbers, for 1990 and 1995.

2. What percentage of visitors in 1995 came from outside Africa?

National Parks and Major Game Reserves

South Africa has 17 national parks, 11 of which provide accommodation facilities. The most famous, the Kruger National Park, supports more mammal species than any other park in Africa, including a great diversity of bird species. Each of the national parks offers an exceptional eco-experience. There are hiking trails in the Golden Gate Highlands National Park, the Augrabies National Park, and the Karoo National Park which also offers trips in four-wheel drive vehicles. Canoe rides are popular in the West Coast National Park.

Other Facilities: All of the main camps have restaurants and shops where provisions, tinned foods and curios may be bought. In addition: picnic spots, filling stations, vehicle workshops, conservation related film shows, information centres, conference facilities, post offices and a bank. Cars may be hired at Skukuza.

1. Kruger National Park	9. Touchstone Game Ranch	17. Royal Natal National Park
2. Londolozi Game Reserve	10. Pilansberg Game Reserve	18. Golden Gate National Park
3. Ngala Game Reserve	11. Itala Game Reserve	19. Addo Elephant National Park
4. Mala Mala/Rattray Reserves	12. Mkuze Game Reserve	20. Tsitsikamma National Park
4. Motswari/M'Bali Game Reserve	13. Phinda Game Reserve	21. Shamwari Game Reserve
4. Sabi Sabi Game Reserve	14. Hluhluwe Game Reserve	22. West Coast National Park
4. Ulusaba Game Reserve	15. Umfolozi Game Reserve	23. Kalahari Gemsbok National Park
8. Kapama Game Reserve	16. Giants Castle Game Reserve	24. Richtersveld National Park

RESOURCE 4.4

National Parks and Major Game Reserves.

The tourism industry then organises the safari holidays into these parks and reserves. Resource 4.5 is taken from a 1997 holiday brochure, and shows how the safaris work. Although some big companies offer safaris, the packages are generally specialised for people interested in viewing wildlife who can afford it.

3. Read through Resource 4.5 carefully. Suppose you have been on this holiday. After you get back, a friend asks some questions, what would your answers be?

 How long did it take you to get there?

 Where did you stay?

 What did you do each day?

 How did you travel around and what did you see?

 How much did it cost?

28 Thatched Rooms and	Excellent Restaurant and	**HIPPO HOLLOW**
Chalets with Balconies,	Wine Cellar	
Braais and River Views	Bar	
Kitchenette with Fridge and	Swimming Pool	
Utensils (no Stove or	FREE Parking	
Microwave)	Other Restaurants,	
Ceiling Fans (Air	Golf, River Rafting, Hot Air	
Conditioning not Necessary	Ballooning Nearby	
with Thatched Roofs)	Welcome Tours Safaris in	
Private Bathrooms — Double	Open Vehicles to Kruger	
Showers, No Baths	Park.	

FULL DAY SAFARI

'Be ready at 7 a.m. – your open 4WD is waiting! We drive first along the banks of the Sabie River, so look out for hippos and crocodiles.

In the Kruger Park your guide will search for 'The Big Five' – lion, elephant, leopard, rhino, buffalo. Back at the lodge in time to watch the sunset, and the animals take an evening drink at the waterhole'

ACCOM CODE 7910			HIPPO HOLLOW				ROOM ONLY
NO NIGHTS	01 APR '97– 31 MAY	01 JUN– 30 JUN	01 JUL– 31 OCT	01 NOV– 09 DEC	10 DEC– 13 JAN '98	14 JAN– 31 MAR	child discount under 12
SIX	819	849	879	889	1109	929	60%
THIRTEEN NIGHTS	1039	1079	1109	1129	1349	1169	60%
EXTRA NIGHTS	23	23	23	23	23	23	75%
SINGLE SUPP	10	10	10	10	10	10	N/A
CAR INCLUDED: EXTRA NIGHT PRICES AND SINGLE SUPPLEMENTS ARE PER PERSON PER NIGHT AND DO NOT INCLUDE CAR HIRE							

DESTINATIONS	OUTWARD					INWARD				
	FLIGHT NO.	DEPARTURE	ARRIVAL	DAYS OF OPERATION	NO. STOPS	FLIGHT NO.	DEPARTURE	ARRIVAL	DAYS OF OPERATION	NO. STOPS
HEATHROW/JOHANNESBURG/ LONDON	VS601	2145	1000*	MON/WED/THUR/ FRI/SAT/SUN	0	VS602	2015	0635*	MON/TUE/THUR/ FRI/SAT/SUN	0

* Arrives the following day

THE KRUGER NATIONAL PARK

The biggest and most popular of the parks is Kruger National Park (Resource 4.4). It covers more than 21 000 km^2 – about the size of Wales – and about 700 000 tourists come each year. Over one-half stay an average of three days. The rest are day visitors who stay in hotels, lodges and camps outside the park.

RESOURCE 4.5
Hippo Hollow.

4. From Resource 4.4:

a) What sort of things can tourists enjoy in the Kruger National Park?

b) Make a list of the jobs supported by the safari tourism.

IS SAFARI TOURISM A GOOD THING?

Safaris help to support at least 50 000 jobs. Many are in remote rural areas where there are few industries. Local people work in the hotels and lodges, act as guides and park rangers, and the tourists buy souvenirs of local crafts. Every extra 11 tourists create one new job. Yet not everyone is happy.

A village elder explains:

OK, so the safaris do give us some jobs and money. But when the government set up the parks and reserves they took away our traditional lands. We used to graze our animals, and hunt. Now we are kept out, because they say the parks and reserves are for the wild animals, so that tourists can see them.

The government has realised the problems and has changed its policy. For example, the new Richtersveld Park lies in the remote, dry west of the country **(Resource 4.4)**. Local people have been involved as the park has developed:

When we first heard that the government was thinking about a park in our homeland, we made sure that they came and talked with us. We set up a committee and put our case to keep our rights to graze and hunt. Now the park is running, we help manage it. All of the ten park rangers are local men. We can graze and hunt in the park less, but have won rights to extra lands outside the park.

Safari tourism is expensive and brings in large amounts of money. Until recently, local people gained little. Today however, in and around the parks and reserves, as in Richtersveld, the local population are becoming more involved. They have a say in managing some parks, more jobs are being created, and their traditional rights are being accepted, or at least considered.

RESOURCE 4.6
Norway as a tourism destination.

Against mass tourism	For specialist tourism
• Cool, wet and often severe climate. No 'Sun-sea-sand' resources!	• Great mountain scenery
• Few roads, settlements and hotels over much of the country	• Fantastic fjord and island coastline
	• Super skiing
• A difficult, rugged landscape	• Friendly people
• Most things, including food, are expensive	• Wild, empty places for walking and camping
• Travel from the main European and American markets is expensive and not always easy	• Fantastic fjord and island coastline
	• Super skiing

CRUISE SHIP TOURISM IN NORWAY

Norway is not a mass tourism destination, but it does have attractive resources for some types of specialist tourism (Resource 4.6). As a result, the country's tourism industry is developing several **niche markets** where Norway can take advantage of its resources to compete successfully. A niche is a particular part or position within the total market. Think again of Lotus cars – they have a special niche in or part of the total car market.

CRUISING NORWAY'S COASTS

Ocean cruising is a good example of a specialist niche in the tourism market. It is also one of the most rapidly growing niches. It is not surprising therefore, that Norway, with its spectacular coastline, is increasingly popular (Resource 4.7).

RESOURCE 4.8
Brochure extract of a Norwegian Coastal voyage.

RESOURCE 4.7 Cruise ship in a fjord.

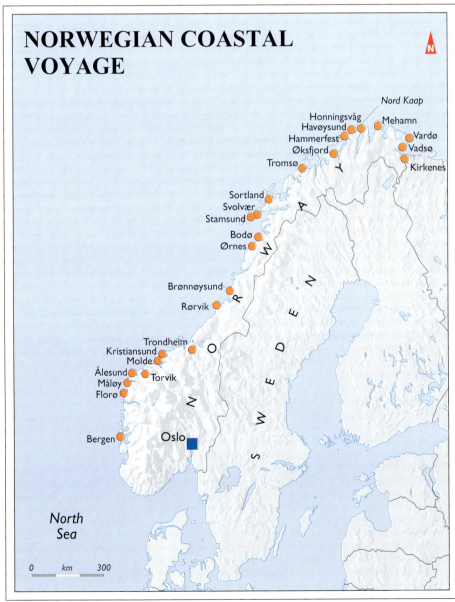

NORWEGIAN COASTAL VOYAGE

Sailing from Bergen, the eleven day round voyage covers 2500 miles and calls at 34 ports, towns and fishing villages. You will enjoy spectacular mountains, glaciers, fjords and islands. Watch out for whales, eagles, reindeer and many other creatures.

DAY 4: Cross the Arctic Circle, entering 'The Land of the Midnight Sun', with views of the Svartisen Glacier. Time for shopping in Bodo, or a trip by bus to the mountain viewpoint at Ronvik.

DAY 6: After sailing at night, we dock at Honningsvag. If you are an early riser, you can join the bus excursion to North Cape. This is a journey through rugged mountains. We take breakfast at the top of the great Nord Kaap cliff, looking out over the ocean.

PRICES per person, Summer 1997
Standard cabin £1630
De luxe cabin £2695
Prices include –
Return flights from the UK.
All meals on board

Cruising attracts a special type of tourist, or **market segment** (See p. 23). Cruises are expensive and most people can afford to spend freely. So the places they visit should benefit. Resource 4.8 is made up of extracts from a brochure for a typical cruise.

Look carefully at Resources 4.7 and 4.8.

5. What resources does Norway have which attract cruise ship tourists?

6. A **market segment** means the type of person who buys a particular type of product. Describe the market segment, i.e. the type of person, the cruise company is trying to attract.

7. A company uses advertising to help sell its products. The colourful brochure is the main way a tour company or country advertises its holiday products. Make a list of the *images* of the cruise and of Norway, being used to 'sell' this product.

8. These are some of the features of specialist tourism – small scale; expensive; high quality accommodation, food, activities and experiences; appeals to limited market segments; has high status or 'snob' value; involves learning about places as well as enjoying them. Which of these features does cruising have?

9. Think of another type of specialist holiday.

   a) Identify the market segment (the type of people) it will appeal to

   b) Produce a brochure page for this holiday. Make sure you present an image which will appeal to the market segment you are aiming at.

TOURISM GOES GLOBAL

5

Key Idea

You can buy a 'Big Mac', a Nissan car or a pair of Reeboks in countries all over the world. Demand for these products is global. And it is not only the demand, many of these companies have offices and factories all over the world, they are multinational companies. This trend is globalisation. It affects demand, supply and the way companies are organised. This chapter looks at how globalisation affects the travel and tourism industry.

RESOURCE 5.1
Tourists travel the world. Thousands of Japanese tourists visit Jasper National Park in Canada every summer.

The global explosion of tourism

The graph in Resource 5.2 shows the huge numbers of international travellers. These are people who travel from their own country to another. Notice how quickly the numbers are growing. This travel is from and to all parts of the world. The majority is within and between Europe and North America (Resources 5.3 and 5.4). These figures include people who travel on business, who visit families and friends, and who go on holiday.

RESOURCE 5.2
More and more people are travelling abroad. World totals of international travellers.

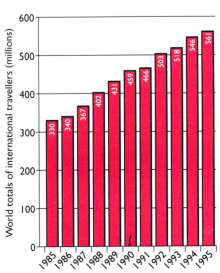

World totals of international travellers (millions)

Year	
1985	330
1986	340
1987	367
1988	402
1989	431
1990	459
1991	466
1992	503
1993	518
1994	546
1995	561

Australia, New Zealand and Pacific islands
Asia
North America
Africa
Central and South America
Europe

RESOURCE 5.3
Where do they all come from? Origins of international travellers in 1994.

RESOURCE 5.4
Where do they all go to?
Arrivals of international travellers in 1994.

Destination	Number (million)
Africa	18
North America (Canada and USA)	79
Central and South America	28
East and South East Asia	70
India, Bangladesh and Pakistan	4
Australia, New Zealand and Pacific Islands	7
Middle East	10
Mediterranean Europe	106
Western Europe	118 Europe 330
Northern, Central and Eastern Europe	106
	TOTAL 546

1. Look at Resource 5.2.

   a) How many international travellers were there in 1985, 1990, 1995?

   b) What were the percentage increases, 1985–90; 1990–1995?

2. Resource 5.2 tells us total numbers, but where do all these travellers come from and go to?

   a) Look at Resource 5.3.

   i. Name the three regions which provide the largest numbers of international travellers. List them in order, greatest number first
   ii. What percentage of travellers begin their journeys in Europe? (The full circle makes up 100 per cent)
   iii. Asia has a much larger population than Europe, but provides a far smaller number of travellers. Suggest two reasons for this.

   b) Use the information in Resource 5.4.

   i. From the table, construct a pie chart. (Resource 5.3 is an example. Use a computer software package if one is available)
   ii. What percentage of the total arrivals are in European countries?
   iii. Name the two most popular destinations outside Europe.
   iv. Suggest two reasons why so many more foreign visitors arrive in North America than in the Indian sub-continent (India, Bangladesh, Pakistan).

Shrinking distances

The main reason for the growing numbers is that travel has become easier and quicker. Sixty years ago, it took up to two months to travel from Britain to Australia. Today we can fly there in one day. For a British family to visit relatives in Delhi (India), the flight time is less than 10 hours. At least 1.6 million people fly within the USA each day. All this is possible because of passenger jet aircraft. Since they were first introduced around 1960, they have become bigger, faster and able to fly longer distances (Resource 5.5). Also, flying has become less expensive. In 1996, the fares per kilometre were about one-half of those in 1960. The world seems smaller as more people fly more often, more quickly, more cheaply and for greater distances. New technology has created a **transport revolution**.

RESOURCE 5.5
The latest Boeing 747 'Jumbo jet'.

Big planes – big money

One reason that air travel has become cheaper per kilometre, is that airlines and aircraft have become larger. This allows a form of **mass production**. An airline manager uses the graph Resource 5.6 to explain how mass production works.

On routes where demand is large enough, e.g. London–Los Angeles or Tokyo (Japan)–Hong Kong, airlines can use 'jumbo' jets with up to 450 seats. To keep up with demand, 'double-decker' jumbos are being designed, which will carry 1000 passengers. Modern jet aircraft are very expensive. In 1996, the price of a new Boeing 747–400 'jumbo' was about £150 million. It is also costly to keep the aircraft flying – and earning money! (Resource 5.7). It is not surprising therefore, that air travel is dominated by a few very big multinational companies. These are known as **mega-carriers** (Resource 5.8). Notice how many people these mega-carriers employ. A typical 747 'jumbo' has a flight crew of 16 people, and flies for 4500 hours a year. It takes eight crews to cover this amount of flying. When all of the ground staff are included, one 747 aircraft supports about 400 jobs.

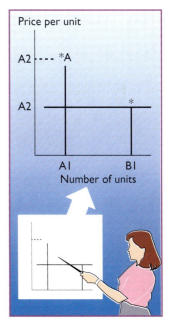

RESOURCE 5.6
A manager explains: if a company can only produce a small number of units (A1), they are likely to be expensive (A2). However, if a company can mass-produce product (B1), the price per unit should be lower.

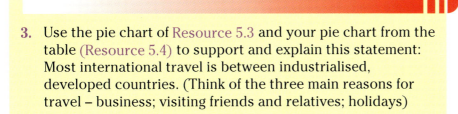

3. Use the pie chart of Resource 5.3 and your pie chart from the table (Resource 5.4) to support and explain this statement: Most international travel is between industrialised, developed countries. (Think of the three main reasons for travel – business; visiting friends and relatives; holidays)

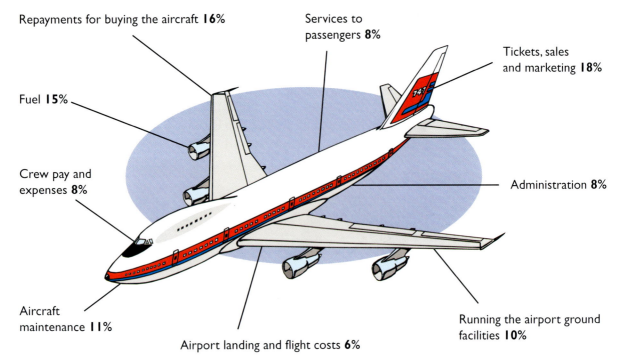

Repayments for buying the aircraft **16%**

Services to passengers **8%**

Tickets, sales and marketing **18%**

Fuel **15%**

Crew pay and expenses **8%**

Administration **8%**

Aircraft maintenance **11%**

Airport landing and flight costs **6%**

Running the airport ground facilities **10%**

RESOURCE 5.7
Costs of running a jumbo jet.

Airline	People employed
American	90 000
United	80 000
Delta	70 000
British Airways	50 000

RESOURCE 5.8
The world's biggest airlines.

4. Study Resource 5.6.

a) Complete this sentence: 'The graph shows that as output increases, so . . .'

b) What is 'mass production' and what are its advantages?

c) The airline manager explains what he means by 'the economies of scale'.

Describe how this idea works for MacDonalds.

5. a) What is the most expensive item in the running of a jumbo jet (Resource 5.7)?

b) The company needs to save money on running costs. Choose **one** item from the list on which you would reduce spending. Explain your choice and how you would do it. What would be the **last** item on which you would try to save money – and why?

6. Two important questions about any business are:

☐ Is it expensive to set up and to run? That is – is it capital intensive?

☐ Does it create a lot of jobs? That is – is it labour intensive?

(Look again at the definitions on page 15)

From the information you have:

a) What facts support the idea that the airline industry is capital intensive?

b) What facts suggest that it is labour intensive?

c) From your sets of facts, is it fair to say that the airline industry is both capital intensive **and** labour intensive? Give reasons for your answer.

Filling the seats to make a profit

If you own a business, the buildings, equipment and employees cost you a lot of money. So you want to use them as efficiently as possible. For an airline, this means two things: first, keep your aircraft flying, because they do not earn money while they are on the ground; second, fill as many of the seats as possible. This is particularly important for long-distance flights which use big, expensive aircraft.

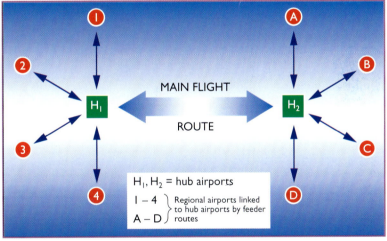

RESOURCE 5.9
Airlines: the hub-and-spoke system allows an airline to increase its seat loading level, that is the percentage of the seats in an aircraft which are filled. The ideal of course, is for a seat loading level of 100 per cent.

All forms of public transport face the problem that there may not be enough demand together at one place. However, a bus can fill up by making frequent stops. A train can stop at several stations. But this is less easy for an aircraft. There are not many airports, and the landing–loading–take off sequence takes a long time.

The airlines' answer has been to develop what they call the 'hub-and-spoke' system (Resource 5.9). Smaller aircraft fly passengers along feeder routes from regional airports (1–4 on Resource 5.10) to a main hub airport (H1). In Britain, regional airports may be Edinburgh, Cardiff, Leeds, Birmingham. London Heathrow is the main hub. At this hub, the passengers are 'sorted' onto the international flights. At the destination hub (H2), such as New York or Rio de Janeiro, some passengers are dispersed by feeder routes to regional airports (A–D)

Can smaller airlines survive?

Because running an airline is so expensive, the most important trend is for the mega-carriers to grow even bigger. Some buy smaller competitors. British Airways bought British Caledonian Airways, which is now one part of BA. Others form partnerships. In 1997, British Airways and American Airways were talking together (look again at Resource 5.8). United Airlines has agreements with British Midland, Thai, SAS, Air Canada, Lufthansa, Varig and Ansett (Australia) airlines.

A director of United Airlines says: 'It makes sense for three reasons. We get the economies of scale. We reduce the competition. We improve our network of routes and places we fly to, and customers like this.'

But in many countries, some smaller airlines have been successful. Virgin Atlantic is a good example. It carefully selected a few popular routes, and built an 'image' based on the owner, Richard Branson (Resource 5.10). Today it is much larger and competes with the mega-carriers.

Another way is to fly routes which are not attractive to the big airlines. These may be shorter routes with limited demand, and can succeed with low cost, smaller aircraft. These companies fill specialised areas or niches of the total market.

RESOURCE 5.10
A Virgin Atlantic advert.

BRITISH AIRWAYS OFFER.	VIRGIN ATLANTIC OFFER.
You must first spend between £250 and £500 at Sainsbury's, to even qualify.	You don't have to spend a penny at Sainsbury's. Just pick up the phone.
Then use the Sainsbury's points that you've collected to qualify for the BA offer.	Keep your Sainsbury's points for something useful, like a toaster.
Get half price fares on British Airways. e.g. New York from £153 return.	Get half price fares on Virgin Atlantic. e.g. New York from £153 return.
You have to take a partner. Minimum two tickets must be purchased.	You can find a partner when you get there. Singles welcome.
There's no choice of in-flight entertainment. You get what you're given.	There's a huge choice of in-flight entertainment. You get your own tv screen.

British and proud of it. |

For half price fares on all Virgin Atlantic routes call 01293 747 238 or see your travel agent by 12 November.

virgin atlantic

RESOURCE 5.11
An Alaska Airlines tailplane with logo.

- British Midland is a regional feeder airline for United Airlines' hub-and-spoke system.
- In North America, Alaska Airways connects smaller and often remote airports (Resource 5.11). A third type survives where a government feels there should be a national airline, i.e. prestige reasons, e.g. Air India, Air Mauritius.

7. Read the 'Can smaller airlines survive?' section carefully. Now think about the car industry. In what ways do smaller car makers have similar opportunities to smaller airlines? Are these niche markets, and if so, give examples?

THE PACKAGE HOLIDAY BUSINESS

Resource 5.12 is taken from the 1997 brochure of a large tour operator. A tour operator is a company which puts together holiday 'packages' – travel, accommodation and activities. We go into a travel agent, study different brochures, and select a package holiday. If you try to book the same holiday for yourself by contacting the airlines, hotels etc. it will cost you much more. Why?

A Thomson Holidays manager explains:

> The answer is – economy of scale. We buy in bulk. We can agree to take several thousand flight seats and hotel rooms each week throughout a season. This means we can bargain for lower fares per seat and cheaper rates per room. The airlines and hotel owners know we are a big company, and can go to other airlines and hotels. We even have our own airline – Britannia Airways. However, we have to pay for the flight seats and the hotel rooms, so we have to advertise hard to sell our holiday packages

One of the most memorable features of Sri Lanka is its warm hospitality. Hardly surprising then that the word 'serendipity', the art of making unexpected and pleasant discoveries, is frequently used when speaking of this island paradise.

Stilt Fisherman in the South of Sri Lanka

Travelwise

Sri Lanka offers a magical combination of history, culture, superb scenery and golden beaches. Hotels tend to be simple, entertainment limited and unsophisticated, service a little slow but prices are amazingly low and everything comes with a disarming smile. There are some excellent beaches but beware of strong undercurrents, particularly May to September, and watersports are not a major pursuit here. A coastal railway runs close to the beach hotels.

Visa required: No. Health: Malaria, Typhoid, Polio, Yellow Fever (if travelling from an infected country), Hepatitis A.

Local Excursions

The following are the three most popular excursions on the island :
Full day tour of Colombo approx. £15
Full day Kandy approx. £39
Full day Galle approx. £32
These trips are bookable and payable locally. Prices may vary depending on the joining point in Sri Lanka.

Special Events

FEB Navam Perahera
APR Sinhala and Tamil New Year
JUL/AUG Esala Festivals
NOV Dambadeniya Perahera
DEC Sangamitta Day
For further information contact the Sri Lanka Tourist Board on 0171 262 5009.

RESOURCE 5.12
Sri Lanka Highlights.

The mass tourism business is risky and very competitive. Look on the shelves of any travel agent and count the number of companies competing for your money.

Companies rely on selling large numbers of holidays at a small profit per holiday. It is not surprising therefore that a few large companies dominate the trade (Resource 5.13).

So, we can explain the global explosion of tourism in terms of demand and supply. Demand is growing because more people have the time, money and interest in travelling. Supply is growing because of large, fast jet aircraft and the economical prices of holiday packages.

RESOURCE 5.13
The British 'package holiday' business.

(Pie chart segments: Thomson, Air Tours, Owners Abroad, Cosmos, Others)

RESOURCE 5.14
Flight delays at Heathrow over a bank holiday.

Limits to growth

Each year there are newspaper photos of overcrowded airports and headlines of long flight delays (Resource 5.14). Major 'hub' airports throughout the world are reaching their capacity. Yet forecasters tell us that air traffic will double within 25 years. A new terminal and runway are being built at London Heathrow. Manchester airport wants to build a second runway (Resource 5.15).

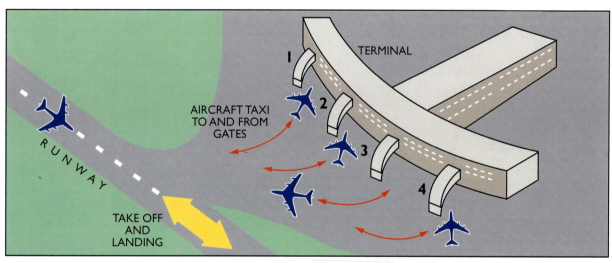

RESOURCE 5.15
An airport at work.

Capacity is important in all industries. It affects the number of jobs and customers as well as the profits of a business. Here are some examples:

- A car factory can be organised to assemble 300 vehicles in a working day. This is its daily output capacity;

- A supermarket checkout counter can deal with an average of 20 customers an hour. If the supermarket is open for 12 hours, and has 20 checkout counters, the customer capacity is $20 \times 12 \times 20 = 4800$.

- A leisure centre may have five squash courts. When each court can be booked for 30 minute sessions, four people can play per hour. If the Centre is open for 10 hours, then the number of people who can play squash each day $= 4 \times 10 \times 5 = 200$. This is the playing capacity.

We measure the capacity of an airport in two ways: first, by how many aircraft can take off and land; second, by how many people can depart and arrive. This is its **handling capacity**. The two factors which control this handling capacity are the runways and the terminal buildings (Resource 5.16).

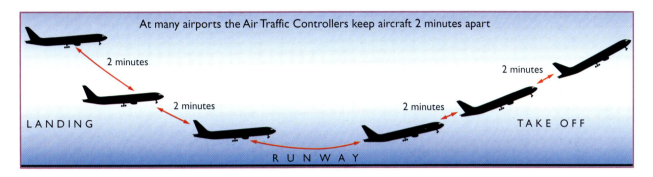

At many airports the Air Traffic Controllers keep aircraft 2 minutes apart

2 minutes — 2 minutes — 2 minutes — 2 minutes

LANDING   RUNWAY   TAKE OFF

Key questions for measuring runway capacity:

- How many runways are there? If there is only one, this will be used for take-offs and landings.

- How long is each runway? This decides the size of aircraft.

- How close together can aircraft be when they take off and land? Safety rules control how close aircraft should be to each other (Resource 5.16).

- For how many hours a day can a runway be used? Major airports are in or near cities, and may be closed at night.

EXAMPLE: 1. An airport has two runways. Each take 'jumbo' jets.
2. The airport is open for 16 hours a day.
3. Aircraft can take off and land at 2 minute intervals.
4. The average number of passengers per aircraft is 130 (This is an average of aircraft of all sizes).

RUNWAY CAPACITY CALCULATION:
60 aircraft per hour (30 take-off; 30 landing)
× 16 hours = 960 aircraft/day
Passenger capacity = 960 × 130 = 124 800 passengers.

8. The average time an aircraft stands at a terminal gate is two hours. In the example of p. 44 the runway capacity is 960 aircraft in 16 hours. The terminals can operate for the full 24 hours. So, how many gates does the airport need?

9. If the airport has two runways, but only 30 gates, suggest **two** ways which managers could avoid delays and overcrowding.

Each space in the daily take-off and landing timetable is known as a 'slot'. Each slot is linked to access to a terminal gate. At popular airports such as London Heathrow or O'Hare Chicago, airlines compete fiercely for these slots and gates. So, a larger, richer airline may buy up a smaller airline for its slots and gates at a certain airport. Also, international agreements control which airlines and how many aircraft can fly a particular route. Governments often favour their own national airlines. British Airways is a British-owned company, and has more slots and gates at London Heathrow than any other airline.

Key questions for measuring terminal capacity (For loading and unloading, an aircraft stands at a terminal 'gate' [1–4 on Resource 5.15]). So:

- How many gates are there?
- How long does an aircraft stand at a gate?
- How many hours a day can a gate be used?

10. You are in charge of a company which has set up a new airline. You have four aircraft, and want to fly a route between Britain and USA.

a) Your first choice is to fly London–New York. What would be the advantages and problems of this choice for your company?

b) Your second choice is to fly between a regional airport in Britain and a similar airport in north-eastern USA. What are the advantages and disadvantages of this second choice for your company? (In both choices, consider demand, supply, capacity, competition, costs, profits)

c) Why might your airline have to start with the second choice?

In this chapter we have learned:

- Demand for many goods and services is increasingly global.
- Production and supply of many goods and services are becoming global, organised by multinational companies.
- Mass production gives economies of scale. This helps to increase output and keep costs and prices down.
- Competition between companies is often fierce. This is why companies try to use their buildings, equipment and workers as near to capacity as possible.
- Capacity is an important control on how a business works.

DEVELOPMENT THROUGH TOURISM

6

Key Idea

Many developing countries are becoming popular destinations for tourism. It can bring great benefits to the country, for example, employment for many people, a greater amount of money being spent in the country. But it can also bring dangers, such as pollution or using too many of the country's natural resources. In this chapter we look at how some places have avoided the pitfalls while others are constantly fighting against them.

What is development?

Juan and his family live beside the River Amazon in Brazil (Resource 6.1). They grow their food, catch fish and eat a healthy diet. Juan says – 'We're lucky because we have our small farm. But we are poor. We have little money. We want a better life' (Resource 6.2).

There are millions of people like Juan, living in what are called Less Economically Developed Countries or LEDCs. These are contrasted with More Economically Developed Countries (MEDCs) such as Britain, Germany, USA, Japan and New Zealand. We say that LEDCs are 'poor', while MEDCs are 'rich'. So as a country becomes developed, it becomes richer. But what do we mean by 'richer'? Development means not just having more money, but more people having better lives. Look again at Juan's hopes in Resource 6.2.

RESOURCE 6.1
An Amazonian farmer at home.

New jobs
New roads
Better schools
Better hospitals
Safe water
Better transport
See other places
More farm equipment
Crops to sell
Bigger house
Different foods
Radio
TV
Bikes
New clothes
Furniture
More money to spend

RESOURCE 6.2
What Juan's family mean by a better life.

Measuring development

One measure for 'rich' and 'poor' is the **national product per person**. Resource 6.3 explains how we calculate this measure. The values for 'rich' MEDCs are high and for 'poor' LEDCs, are low. However, this is only one way we can see differences in levels of development. For example, it does not tell us *who* is rich or poor in a country. The list in Resource 6.4 shows some important contrasts between a developed and a less developed country.

RESOURCE 6.3

Measuring 'rich' and 'poor'.

Stage 1: Add up the value of what a country produces each year. This is the **national product**

Stage 2: Find out how many people there are in the country. This is the **population total**

Stage 3: Divide the National Product by the total population:

$$\frac{\text{NATIONAL PRODUCT}}{\text{POPULATION TOTAL}}$$

This gives the value of the National Product per person for that year. The higher this value, the richer the country is said to be

EXAMPLE: National Product = US$ 2000 million
Population total = 2 million

RESOURCE 6.4

Comparing 'rich' and 'poor'.

	LEDC Kenya	MEDC New Zealand
1. Population total (million)	26	3.5
2. National Product per person (US$)	250	15 000
3. People living in towns and cities (% of all people)	27	86
4. Type of jobs (% of all jobs): Farming	80	10
Industry	7	25
5. Children who die before their 1st birthday (number from every 1000 children born)	59	7
6. How long people live, on average (years)	59	76
7. Families who have a safe water supply (% of all families)	53	97
8. Exports from the country (US$ million)	1600	12 500
9. Imports to the country (US$ million)	2200	12 500

1. Look carefully at each measure in Resource 6.4. Compare the figures for Kenya and New Zealand. Make a list, numbered 1–9, and write against each measure, whether the Kenya figure is HIGHER or LOWER than the figure for New Zealand.

2. Use measures 3 and 4 to write two sentences, describing where most people live and how they make their living in
a) Kenya; b) New Zealand.

3. In what ways do the figures for measures 5, 6, 7 suggest that people in New Zealand have better lives than people in Kenya?

4. Look at measures 8 and 9. The balance between the value of exports and imports is a kind of budget. A country gains money by selling products for export. It can then use some of this money to pay for imports. No country wants imports to cost a lot more than income from exports. MEDCs have a range of industries which sell products for export so that they can afford to pay for imports. One feature of LEDCs is that they have only a few products to sell for export. Yet to develop, they need to import lots of materials and goods. Use the figures for measures 8 and 9 to show how this budget balance problem works for Kenya and New Zealand.

RESOURCE 6.5
New industries help development.

Looking for development

Development means: that ideally life gets steadily better for *all* the people of a country. This may take a long time and will cost huge sums of money. Just think of what a government would have to do to make Juan's dreams come true (Resource 6.2).

An LEDC needs more industry. Follow the arrows through Resource 6.5 and you will see two things happening as industries develop. First, demand grows *inside* the country. Second, increased exports bring in more money. This can pay for imports or can be invested in new roads, schools, and other industries.

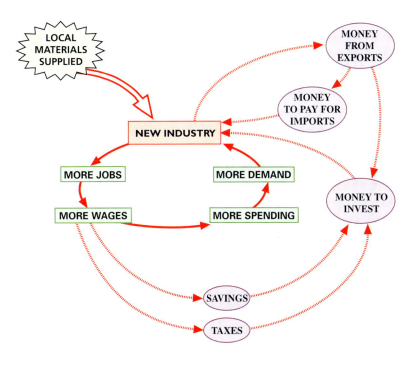

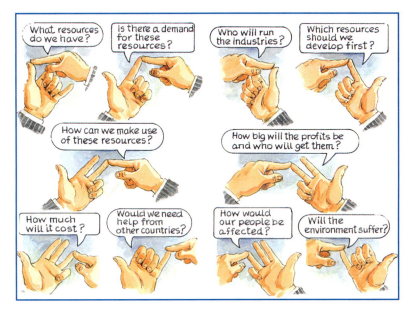

RESOURCE 6.6
Making choices about development.

RESOURCE 6.7
Resources which attract tourists.

This is what government hopes for. However, it needs to encourage industries which are likely to succeed. Making this choice means asking some important questions (Resource 6.6).

Using tourism for development

The tourism industry has been a popular choice by LEDCs.

There are several reasons for this choice:

- Demand has continued to grow rapidly;
- Many LEDCs have resources which are attractive to tourists (Resource 6.7);
- It does not need huge costs to get tourism started;
- Tourism provides plenty of jobs. It is **labour intensive**;
- Spending by international tourists brings in foreign currency which LEDCs need;
- International travel companies encourage tourism development in new places.

5. Use Resource 6.5 to describe what happens when a factory making T-shirts opens in an LEDC. The factory employs 100 people; the cotton is grown and made into cloth locally.

6. The government committee in Resource 6.6 is trying to decide which industries they should encourage. For each question, write down why you think it is an important question and how it could affect the choice.

Case Study: *The Seychelles*

THE IMAGE

More than 80 000 tourists go to the Seychelles each year. One tour company attracts them with this image in their brochure:

'Lush tropical islands lapped by the gleaming turquoise waters of the Indian Ocean. Combine this with powdery white sand beaches shaded by coconut palms and you have the hallmark of these unique islands. Our opinion: the Seychelles offer some beautifully deserted beaches and spectacular tropical scenery. We highly recommend island hopping to some of the smaller islands from Mahé' (*KUONI*, 1997)

THE REALITY

The brochure makes it sound easy to set up a tourism industry – simply advertise 'sun-sea-sand' and palm trees in a tropical paradise, and the tourists will arrive! However, look at Resource 6.8, and you can see that much more is needed. Think of what you enjoy doing when you are on holiday.

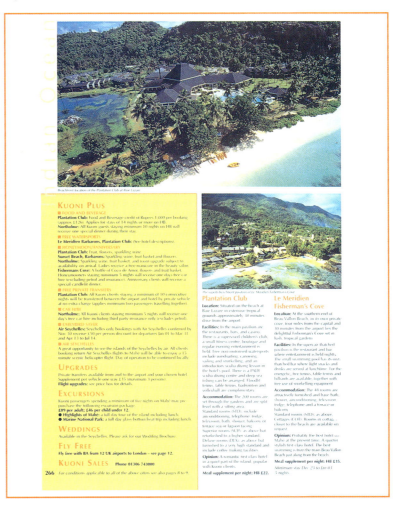

RESOURCE 6.8
Supplying what tourists demand.

Read carefully what the brochure says.

7. Where are the Seychelles and what are they?

8. Make a list of the attractions for tourists.

9. What does the brochure *not* tell you about the Seychelles?

10. Use Resource 6.8 to make lists of things which must be provided for the three parts of a holiday.
   List A – Transport (flying there, landing, travelling around the islands).
   List B – Accommodation, food and drink.
   List C – Activities (enjoying yourself while you are there).

THE PROBLEM

What do we need?

The tourism industry needs airports, roads, hotels, marinas, electricity and water supplies. These are all expensive to build and to run. They need a big construction industry with equipment and skilled engineers. They need good managers and many well-trained workers.

RESOURCE 6.9

Map of the Seychelles.

What do we have?

The Seychelles is a series of small islands (Resource 6.9). In 1970, when the government started to encourage tourism, the population was less than 60 000. People lived by farming and fishing (Resource 6.10). Most jobs were on the tea and coconut plantations. The only exports were tea and coconut oil. There was a small airfield, few paved roads, little electricity, simple water supplies, and no large hotels. There were only 3000 tourists.

By 1995, the Seychelles had an international airport, at least 20 large modern hotels, good electricity and water supplies, and all kinds of 'fun facilities'. These numbers show how important tourism is:

- The 80 000 tourists spend £65 million. At least 50 per cent of this stays in the islands;
- Tourism makes up more than one-quarter of the National Product;
- Out of 25 000 jobs, 8500 are connected with tourism;
- Every 10 extra tourists create one new job.

RESOURCE 6.10 Traditional farming landscape in the Seychelles.

How was it done?

Like many LEDCs, the Seychelles did not have enough money or all the skills to develop large scale tourism. So they looked for international help. For example:

- Grants and loans from foreign aid agencies and banks. The money has been used to build the airport, roads and the electricity and water systems;

- Large multinational civil engineering companies have built the airport, roads etc.;

- Foreign companies, especially from South Africa and Britain, have paid for, own and run the large hotels;

- British advisers and teachers have set up courses to train Seychelles people for jobs in the tourism industry.

RESOURCE 6.11
Has tourism brought development?

> Tourism is a success. Its our largest industry. It brings in one-half of all our foreign money. And look at all the jobs! Most restaurants, gift shops, taxis, boats and watersports businesses are owned by local people. The hotels buy our crops and the fish we catch. Our people have more money to spend, so this helps shopkeepers. The government gets more money from taxes, so we can build more schools and health clinics, and help people improve their homes. We learn about other countries, and people all over the world now know about the Seychelles. Young people don't have to leave the islands to find jobs.

> Oh, I agree that life is much better for many people. But I am worried because the tourism industry is not really ours. The big hotels are owned by foreign companies who take most of the profits. Foreigners have many of the better paid jobs. Tourists pay foreign companies for their holidays. The government took out huge loans to help build the airport and roads. Now we have to pay these loans back. Altogether, at least half the money from tourism is leaking away.

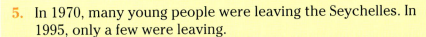

5. In 1970, many young people were leaving the Seychelles. In 1995, only a few were leaving.

    a) You are 18 years old, and the year is 1970. Complete this sentence – 'I am leaving the Seychelles because . . .'

    b) You are 18 years old, and the year is 1995. Complete this sentence – 'I am staying in the Seychelles because . . .'

6. Like many LEDCs, the Seychelles has had to use foreign money and companies to help its industries grow.

    a) Give two reasons for this.

    b) Name two ways the foreign help was used.

    c) Give three benefits the foreign help has brought (Read carefully what the government official says).

7. What does the local teacher mean when she says 'the tourism industry is not really ours'?

8. The local teacher says that money 'leaks away' from the Seychelles. This money is not used within the islands to help development.

   a) Name three ways that the money from tourism leaks away.

   b) Why would both the government official and the teacher hope that leakage can be reduced?

RESOURCE 6.12
Belize fact-file.

An alternative path: an example from Belize

Many LEDCs are asking these questions:

- ▢ Can we start up industries without needing lots of money?
- ▢ Can we keep control of the new industries?

The answers include:

- ▢ Small businesses which local people can afford, and are able to run;
- ▢ Local people own the businesses and keep most of the profits;
- ▢ Industries which can succeed without expensive buildings and high technology.

Belize is a small country, about the size of Wales. It has a population of about 350 000. Most people live in villages and farm small plots of land. They are **subsistence farmers**, that is they grow much of their own food. The natural vegetation is tropical rainforest.

Average earnings are low and Belize needs to develop new industries. Exports are mainly oranges, bananas, grapefruit and pineapples, grown on large farms and plantations. Tourism is one of the new industries encouraged by the government.

In Belize, a small country in Central America, a group of villages have taken these ideas to develop tourism (Resource 6.12). A few years ago the villagers of Bermudan Landing were cutting down the rainforest to make more farmland. A visiting scientist noticed that a number of rare Black Howler Monkeys lived in these forests. He told the villagers that tourists would come to see these monkeys. This would mean keeping [conserving] some of the forest, but would bring money and some jobs.

The local people call the Howler Monkeys 'baboons'. The Belize government and the World Wildlife Fund for Nature (WWFN) helped with money and advice and the villagers set up the Community Baboon Sanctuary (Resource 6.13).

The Manager explains – 'We have a committee of villagers to manage the Sanctuary. We did not have the skills at first, so the WWFN gave us advice. They also helped us build this Visitor Centre. I have trained some young local men to be guides. They meet the tourists here and take them on walks through the forest where they will get close to the monkeys. We charge about £3 for a guided walk and sell T-shirts, posters and booklets. We now get about 6000 visitors a year. We began with one village and now eight villages have joined our scheme.'

RESOURCE 6.13
The visitor centre.

A Guide says: 'I work on my family farm and am a part-time guide. It gives me some extra money and I get to meet all sorts of people. The manager trained me and a scientist taught me about the Howlers. I understand now how we can conserve the forest for the monkeys as well as making money for ourselves. Each family of five or six monkeys needs several acres of forest to find enough food. Since we started the Sanctuary the number of Howlers has doubled, so that is good. I know their habits and so can get the tourists close to them.'

RESOURCE 6.14
The Howler monkeys.

RESOURCE 6.15
A family farm takes tourists.

A Tourist says: 'We are staying in this family farmhouse. Our room is not luxurious, but has great views into the forest. We eat with the family and are learning a lot about their lives. They still farm, and also make extra money from the tourists. It costs us about £15 each to stay here for a night, including food. The family is using some of their money to put in a shower, and to buy bikes for the kids. John, the father, is on the Sanctuary committee and is very proud of what they have done. He wants to attract more tourists, but is afraid that if the scheme gets too big, a foreign company might want to take over.'

9. Running the Community Baboon Sanctuary is hard work. Give reasons why most villagers feel the effort is worth it.

10. This type of tourism is an alternative to mass tourism. Describe what the tourists do and enjoy when they visit the Sanctuary.

11. Describe the ways the local people are involved in the tourism industry.

12. Little of the money from tourism 'leaks' from the villages. Explain why this leakage is so low.

    (Look again at what causes money to 'leak' away – pp. 51–52)

13. Give two important ways in which tourism in Belize is different from tourism in the Seychelles.

INDUSTRY AND THE ENVIRONMENT

Key Idea

All industries make an impact on the environment. We need to think carefully about how we can reduce and control these impacts.

Counting the costs

All economic activities have *some* effect on the environment:

- a farmer removes trees and ploughs up grassland to plant crops;
- a company builds a factory which takes up land and causes some air pollution;
- a government constructs roads which help industry, but which affect the countryside.

There are many examples within the tourism industry. Even going to the beach affects the environment. (Resource 7.1).

So, economic activities will always cause environmental changes. We must remember that not all these changes will be bad; some may improve the environment. This chapter helps you to think about how we can control the changes and impacts.

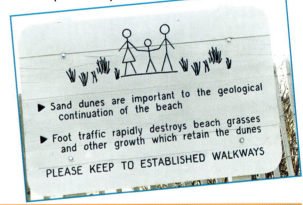

RESOURCE 7.1
Environmental impacts of tourism. A State Park in Maine, USA.

1. Look carefully at Resource 7.1. Describe briefly the environmental impacts caused by tourism on this beach.

Changing attitudes

Today there are more than 5 billion people in the world. Every one of them hopes for a better standard of living. To do this, more resources will be used and environments will continue to change. But how can we control and manage this change?

In the rush to industrialise, to have more jobs and more money, the effects and impacts have often been ignored. One result has been serious damage and pollution (Resource 7.2). Today we think more carefully about the effects of what we do. We consider the **environmental impacts** of economic activity. We have not solved all the problems, but at least efforts are being made.

RESOURCE 7.2
Careless industry brings pollution.

Nuclear take-over of East Europe

The Rivers Ran Black

A huge oil spill fouls Russia's far north
[TIME, 7-11-94]

Paradise Polluted

In South Korea's latest disaster, a fierce typhoon wrecks an oil tanker and befouls a scenic coast
[TIME, 7-8-95]

Alarm as bathers get ill at 'safe' beaches

BATHERS have caught sewage-related illnesses on two of Britain's cleanest tourist beaches, unpublished government research reveals.

The disturbing revelations, at the start of the summer season, suggest that hundreds of British beaches previously regarded as safe could pose a health risk to holidaymakers.

Water quality scientists, warned that the results undermined the Blue Flag and Seaside awards given by the European Community and the Tidy Britain Group to help the public choose clean, safe beaches.

Tests conducted for the environment department at Lyme Regis, Cobb and Paignton last August found that bathers were twice as likely to suffer pollution-related ailments including nausea, diarrhoea, vomiting and fever than people who stayed on the beach.

[OBSERVER, 5 JULY 1992]

The tourism industry is a special case. To sustain success, the industry must maintain a high quality environment. For example, seaside resorts need clean beaches and unpolluted water (Resource 7.3). Think again of the safari and cruise tourism we studied in Chapter 4. Tourists will only come while there is varied wildlife and beautiful scenery. However, balancing conservation and development is often difficult, as the example of the Galapagos Islands shows.

RESOURCE 7.3
Beach quality and pollution.

2. In your own local area: **i.** Locate one new or recent business development, e.g. industrial park; shopping centre; offices; leisure/entertainment centre. **ii.** Describe the economic activities that take place. **iii.** Write a brief report or draw a labelled sketch to show what has been done to control the impacts and improve the environment, e.g. tree and lawn landscaping.

Conflict in the Galapagos Islands

The Galapagos Islands, in the eastern Pacific Ocean, are part of Ecuador (Resource 7.4). They have become famous because of their unique wildlife (Resource 7.5). Scientists have learned much about evolution by studying the differences between the animals on the various islands. Today, tourism is the main industry, but not everyone is happy as the viewpoints of four people show.

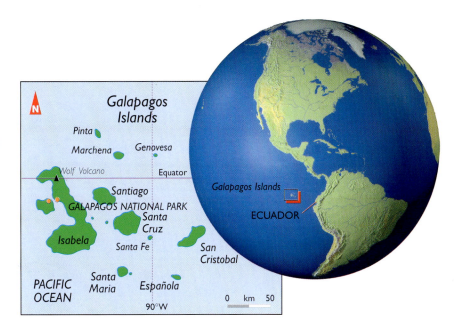

RESOURCE 7.4
Ecuador and the Galapagos.

RESOURCE 7.5
Galapagos Isles: iguanas and tourists.

3. Read the views of the four people carefully.

4. Write two sentences which describe the main problem facing the Galapagos Islands.

5. What has the government done and why is it suggested that this policy is not working?

6. What do you think should be done? Write briefly what you would do, and give reasons for your choice.

RESOURCE 7.6
Four different opinions.

Government Tourist Official

We know the Galapagos are very special. Many species, the iguanas and turtles for example, are found nowhere else on earth. Even the separate islands have their own sub-species. It's not surprising that tourists want to come. Ecuador is a poor country, and our population is growing quickly. We see that tourism will bring jobs and money. The island vegetation and wildlife are easily disturbed. So, we have several policies to protect them. First, we have created a National Park which covers most of the islands. Second, in our national plan for tourism, we set a limit of 25 000 visitors a year. Third, we ban hotels on the islands away from the main town. Tourists sleep and eat on the cruise boats.

National Park Ranger

We have four big problems. First, the government wants more money, so lets more tourists come each year. Second, we don't have enough money. For example, with only two patrol boats it's difficult to control where the boats and the tourists go. Also, we can't employ people to do conservation work on the islands. Third, the people who run the cruises want to give their customers the best experience. So, for example, they often let the tourists get too close to the animals and in too large numbers. We have a 'code of conduct' which the tour guides are supposed to follow, but not everyone obeys. The fourth problem is that many people do not like the National Park. To them, we are taking away their chances of jobs because we try to limit tourist numbers, and prevent developments on islands in the National Park.

Environmentalist

We are very worried. The government plan to limit tourist numbers is not working. We believe well over 40 000 tourists travel around the islands each year. Most come on cruises from mainland Ecuador. These tour operators are getting more permits than they should. The government does not enforce the limits. There are also tour and private boats from California and Mexico. It's very difficult to control them. Then there's pressure from many people on the islands. To them, more tourists mean more jobs and more money. The result is that the wildlife and vegetation are threatened. For example, tourists can disturb animals and birds during their breeding season, so fewer are born and survive. If we don't control tourist numbers, then there won't be these unique iguanas, turtles, finches and so on for people to look at. What would happen to the tourism industry then?

Local Politician

The National Park is a big mistake. Each year, hundreds of poor people come to the Galapagos from all over Ecuador. They hear about the tourism boom and think there will be plenty of jobs. When they can't find work, they become unhappy and angry. It is expensive for our town – we have more police because there is more crime; our health and schools services can't cope. Without the National Park, we could have more tourists, more hotels on the islands and more trips on boats. All this would mean more jobs and more money. It's rubbish to say the iguanas and turtles are more important than people!

Learning how to behave

If you go on holiday to any of the places mentioned in this book, there will be controls on what you do, and how the tourism businesses work. The strongest controls are **laws** and **regulations**. These tell us what **MUST** and **MUST NOT** be done. For example, some countries have laws controlling the hours bars and nightclubs can open. Planning laws control the location and design of hotels (Resource 7.7).

RESOURCE 7.7
On some tropical islands, planning laws say that new hotels must be set back from the beach, be screened by a fringe of trees, and be no taller than the trees.

Less powerful, but increasingly popular, are **guidelines** and **codes of conduct**. These advise us what to do and how to behave. They are produced by governments, businesses and pressure groups such as Greenpeace. The advice may be for tourists or for tourism businesses. The idea is to persuade us to *choose* to look after the environments we are visiting and businesses are working in. Two examples illustrate this approach.

EXAMPLE 1: THOMSON HOLIDAYS (RESOURCE 7.8)

Thomson is Britain's largest tour operator. This is included in their 1997–1998 brochure.

RESOURCE 7.8
The Thomson code.

Environment

Thomson is committed to caring for the environment and the communities in which we operate. We actively encourage our staff, at home and abroad, to support environmental protection at a local level.

For example, the paper used for this brochure is made from trees grown as a commercially renewable resource. For every tree felled to make the paper, two are planted to replace it.

You too can 'do your bit' for the environment when you're on holiday, considerably reducing the pressures that tourism brings to holiday resort areas:

SAVE WATER

GUARD AGAINST FIRE

TURN OFF LIGHTS

PROTECT WILDLIFE

DO NOT LITTER

EXAMPLE 2: THE GOVERNMENT OF NEPAL (RESOURCE 7.9)

The Himalayan country of Nepal is popular for trekking holidays in beautiful, high mountain scenery. Two environmental problems are:

- **Deforestation** and **erosion**. Trekkers stay in villages, and this brings in money. The villagers have built simple hot showers for the tourists. However, wood is burned to heat the water. As more and more trees are removed from the steep slopes, erosion is becoming serious.

- **Litter pollution.** Some trekkers leave litter along the trails. As numbers grow, so the problem gets worse. One popular route is known as 'the Kleenex trail'!

MINIMUM IMPACT CODE

As visitors and friends, we invite you to help conserve the sanctity and beauty of the Annapurna region for generations to come. Here's how to 'step gently' in this fragile area, and make your visit a positively memorable one. We ask that you:

• CONSERVE FIREWOOD. Be self-sufficient in your fuel supply and make sure your trekking staff uses kerosene and has enough warm clothing. Make no open fires. Limit hot showers. If possible, stay at lodges that use kerosene or fuel efficient wood stoves and space heaters.

• STOP POLLUTION. Dispose of all trash properly: Paper products, cigarette butts, toilet paper, food scraps etc. should be burned or buried. Bottles, plastics and other

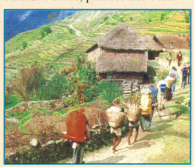

NEPAL IS HERE TO CHANGE YOU, NOT FOR YOU TO CHANGE NEPAL.

non-biodegradable items should be packed out or deposited in rubbish pits if available. Use toilet facilities provided – if none exist, make sure you are 20 metres from any water source and carry a small shovel to bury wastes. Don't use soap or shampoo in any stream or hot spring.

Above all, remember that your vacation has a great impact on the natural environment and people who live off its resources. By assisting in these small ways, you will help the land and people of Nepal enormously. THANK YOU!

RESOURCE 7.9
The trekkers' code in Nepal.

Read the two examples carefully (Resources 7.8–7.9)

1. What environmental impacts are caused by tourism?

2. What are **a)** tourists and **b)** tourism businesses and workers advised to do to reduce environmental impacts?

3. Give two reasons why these codes of conduct may not be successful.